WILFRED OWEN

WILFRED
OWEN
Merryn Williams

Border Lines Series Editor

John Powell Ward

SEREN BOOKS

SEREN BOOKS is the book imprint of
Poetry Wales Press Ltd
Andmar House, Tondu Road, Bridgend, Mid Glamorgan

British Library Cataloguing in Publication Data

Williams, Merryn
Wilfred Owen. — (Border Lines Series)
I. Title II. Series
821.912

ISBN 1-85411-098-5
1-85411-090-X paperback

Cover Illustration: Wilfred Owen, officer cadet, July, 1916
(The Owen Collection, English Faculty Library, Oxford)

*Published with the financial support of the
Welsh Arts Council*

Printed in Palatino by The Cromwell Press, Melksham

Contents

List of Illustrations

1. Wilfred as a soldier, aged about 3

2. Wilfred the student at Reading , aged about 19

3. At Dunsden Vicarage, early 1912

4. With Laurant Tailhade, France, September 1914

5. The Owen family in 1913: Harold, Susan, Colin, Tom, Mary

6. Siegfried Sassoon

7. Wilfred with Arthur Newboult, July 1917

8. Wilfred, the last photograph, late August 1918

9. 'The Canal, Uffington Village' by Harold Owen

10. The Sambre and Oise Canal, November 1918

11. Prophetic cartoon by Will Dyson: Clemenceau leaves the Versailles Conference

12. 'Ecstasy of Fumbling' (1991) by Gulf War artist John Keane

The harps to which we sang are hung
On willow boughs, and their refrain
Drowned by the anguish of the young
Whose blood is mingled with the rain.

Hedd Wynn (Ellis Humphrey Evans) killed 1917
trans. Alan Llwyd)

In memory of my great uncle, George Dalling,
(killed 1915, Gallipoli)
and of Riyadh and Rafal,
lost in the Gulf

Preface

"In August 1914, when the moon was red, I used to go up at night to a hill-top, and look at Spain", Wilfred Owen wrote to his sister in 1917. "I still do that in dreams" (Letter 516). If he had seen the Great War coming, he told her, he might have crossed the mountains into Spain, and escaped his destiny.

Reading these words, I was reminded of a slightly younger poet, then living at the other end of the peninsula, Federico Garcia Lorca, whose name is forever associated with a later war. If Owen had survived, as he so nearly did, he could have expected to see the Spanish Civil War, the Second World War, possibly Vietnam. He would probably not have seen the many 'little' wars of the eighties and nineties, but his words still apply to them: "None will break ranks, though nations trek from progress" — a line which haunted me as this nation moved, "with eyes open and mind closed", towards the second Gulf War.

This book was commissioned for Owen's hundredth birthday. Since he died, English poetry has gone through seventy-five years of irreversible changes; the literary tradition which formed him has been more or less thrown away. But his poetry does not date; indeed it gets more popular as time goes on. Others have written great war poems; he is the great war poet. His spirit seems to brood over a century in which violence, not just between armies but against whole populations, has become the norm. The name Sarajevo, so loaded in his time, has a sinister new meaning in the 1990s. Someone told his friend Sassoon that the war was about "Mesopotamian oil wells" (*Memoirs of an Infantry Officer* [1930], 10, 1) and that sounds familiar, too.

Yet he did not seek the kind of fame he got; at first he bitterly resented the war because it interfered with his writing. As his contemporary, Vera Brittain, recorded in *Testament of Youth* (1933):

> I had begun, I thought, by feeling exasperated about the War, and I went on by ignoring it; then I had to accept it as a fact, and at last was forced to take part in it, to endure the fear and sorrow and fatigue that it brought me, and to witness in impotent anguish the deaths.... It's my job, now, to find out all about it, and try to prevent it, in so far as one person can, from happening to other people in the days to come.... Perhaps the means of salvation are already there, implicit in history, unadvertised, carefully concealed by the warmongers, only awaiting rediscovery (471).

Or as Owen put it, "Yet these elegies are to this generation in no sense consolatory. They may be to the next. All a poet can do today is warn".

This book describes how a young man from an obscure border town became the great poet of the first great modern war. I call him Wilfred in Chapter 1, Owen in Chapter 2, because they are two different entities; Wilfred died, Owen lives. Chapter 3 attempts to draw some threads together and put him in a wider context. It may seem strange that I refer to Bosnia and the Gulf when writing about a poet who died in 1918, but, as Dylan Thomas said, he is a poet of "all times, all places, and all wars". I have tried to show how other poets in the desert, the jungle and the South Atlantic all found him relevant.

Since the first book about Owen came out in 1960, there has been a great deal of valuable work on his life and poetry. I am very conscious of standing on the shoulders of earlier writers, who are acknowledged in the bibliography. I am also grateful to Judith Kazantzis and John Keane for allowing me to reproduce their work, to William Hetherington (Peace Pledge Union), Graham Martin, Helen McPhail, Cambridge University library, Oxford English Faculty library, Shrewsbury reference library, and, as always, my husband.

The text used is *Wilfred Owen: The Complete Poems and Fragments* (ed. Jon Stallworthy, 1983), except for a small number of poems where I an alternative version made better poetry.

M.W.

1: LIFE

The border town of Oswestry has a long history of conflict.Man has lived there since about 550 BC, the date of the Iron Age hill fort; it saw a great battle between Christians and pagans in the seventh century and later many more between Welsh and Normans, and it was wholly or partly destroyed by King John, Llewellyn Fawr, Owain Glyndwr and Cromwell. Having been frequently burned down, it has few buildings from before the nineteenth century. It is a small place, but gave birth to two famous men, Walford Davies, Master of the King's Musick, in 1869, and Wilfred Edward Salter Owen on 18 March 1893.

The house, Plas Wilmot, belonged to his maternal grandfather Edward Shaw, a retired ironmonger and former mayor of Oswestry. Both sides of the family had originally come from across the border. The poet's father, Tom, liked to think he was descended from Baron Lewis Owen, a sheriff of Merionethshire in the sixteenth century, but he himself was a tailor's son, and worked as a clerk on the Great Western Railway. When he met the gently-reared Susan Shaw they could not afford to get married and Tom went to India for several years to try to better himself. He would miss the far east, and the sea, for the rest of his life. But when Susan's father got into financial trouble he came back to marry her and moved into her family home.

Although he had a very meagre salary, then and in future, their lifestyle was way above what he could have afforded. Wilfred, an only child for three years, spent his infancy surrounded by doting adults in a delightful roomy house with a large tree-filled garden, orchards, stables, a croquet lawn and plenty of prize geese and ducks to play with. There is a photograph of him as a small boy, dark-haired and solemn-faced, in a soldier's uniform made by his mother, who had no way of knowing that the 1890s were a particularly bad time to have a son. This blissful life ended in 1897 when old Mr Shaw died deep in debt and the house was sold, the proceeds being shared between his three daughters. The Owens kept the piano and some silver and linen, which they carried into the much smaller houses they would live in thereafter. Wilfred thought of Plas Wilmot as a lost paradise, and when as an adult he bought ivory hairbrushes and oak furniture he may have been dimly recalling a more gracious and ordered way of life.

By this time he had a sister, Mary, and in the next three years two more boys, Harold and Colin, were born. The family moved to Birkenhead and "it was in this period", to quote Harold, "that the acute lack of money began to exert its insidious influence upon our home" (JFO, I, 18). In the 1960s Harold would publish the three-volume *Journey from Obscurity*, one of the great literary autobiographies of the century. It shows us the boy Wilfred as he appeared to a younger brother who did not always much like him, but it also gives a rounded picture of his family's life before the war.

He remembered Birkenhead as dank, slummy place where the Owens were welcomed to their new home by a tribe of black beetles and where unmentionable terrors lurked outside. For the rest of their childhood, they lived on not only the Welsh-English border but also, in Harold's haunting phrase, "the borderline of insufficiency" (JFO, I, 124). There was never quite enough to eat, never quite enough space. The children soon began to look rickety and pinched and were often ill. Anything that could be spared went on school fees and nice clothes, for their parents were anxious to draw a line between them and the children of the underclass

> tiny ones with ancient faces, wizened by constant hunger, sent by their parents to steal pieces of coal. These under-sized little humans with matchstick legs and arms showed astounding cunning, and the eyes of them all ... had the brilliant wariness of rodents. (JFO I, 64)

They lived in a mean district where they were obviously out of place and were pounced on by the local boys when they went out.

In this environment Wilfred grew up rapidly and was often left in charge of the younger children. Harold remembers how, "only a small child himself", he "trotted back and forth with endless glasses of water and held me up"(JFO I, 60) during an illness. Popular psychologists say that the eldest child tends to be well-behaved, a high achiever, one who sticks to the rules. Wilfred fits that pattern; much of his early life was directed towards being the kind of person his mother and teachers wanted. His friend Alec Paton, who spent a holiday with him in the Vale of Clwyd when he was twelve, remembered how conscientiously he read his Bible passage at the end of each day.

While he had a strong protective instinct and loved the younger children (especially the baby, Colin) another part of him wanted to retreat from his family into the ever fascinating world of books. We hear of him sitting up late in a cold bedroom to learn poetry, accusing Harold of "wasting time in hog-like slumber". He was a very favourite pupil at the Birkenhead Institute, the best school his parents could afford:

> his attractive appearance (not to be confused with good looks), his thick dark brown hair and small delicacy of build — perhaps a lack of robustness even — gave him an air of over-adultness.... In all my recollections of Wilfred when he was at school I can never recall any impression of a school-boy: I can only think of him — even when he was only eleven or twelve dressed in school clothes with a schoolboy satchel on his back — as a student. (JFO I, 85)

Physically he took after his father, a small round-faced man; emotionally, he was his mother's child. Tom Owen had bravely given up his dreams of a more adventurous life and settled down in a job he did not much like, to support his family. He felt he had no choice but to make his sons leave home and start earning as soon as possible, although they could only expect dead-end jobs. Susan, unlike her husband, had led a sheltered life and was extremely religious. Much of her spare time was spent on temperance societies and missions to convert the heathen, causes which the grown-up Wilfred did not support. She was also fond of talking about self-sacrifice, a concept which sank deep into the souls of some of her children. She had been a very beautiful woman in her youth, and her family (apart from Harold) adored her.

To post-Freudians, Susan's faults are obvious. She favoured Wilfred at the expense of her other children; she probably drove a wedge between him and his father; she had an irritating habit of sitting back and expecting God to provide. Yet she was probably a nicer person than she appears in Harold's memoir. Her great-nephew, David Gunston, remembers her as an old lady who loved children and plied them with cakes and presents:

> she found unending pleasure in simple things, little things — babies, children, flowers, birds, fish, pot-plants, orna-ments, butterflies, teacups. Her front drawing-room was an untouched Victorian sanctum, almost full of green things which she treated as children, tenderly and admiringly (*The Lady*, 6-12 November 1990).

It is also true that without her, Wilfred might have been pushed into a dreary job at the age of fourteen. She believed him to be capable of great things, and although he did not achieve greatness in the way she hoped, who can say she was wrong? She nourished his imagination by making clerical costumes for him to dress in (she hoped he might really be a clergyman some day) and encour-aging the reading that meant so much to him. Tom saw no future in this and would have liked to get him involved in more 'manly' activities, so Wilfred grew up unnaturally devoted to Susan and believing his father was a philistine. Harold Owen insists that, despite these tensions, they were basically a happy family. They would have been happier if they had not been "perpetually living on the borderline of poverty" (JFO II, 192).

In 1907 the Owens moved south to Shrewsbury, where Tom had been made Assistant Superintendent for the Joint Railways. "Be-ware of the somnolent sluggishness of Shrewsbury" (JFO II, 229), Wilfred would say. If he revisited the town now it would be a culture-shock, with the traffic thronging its steep streets and the pulling-down of many fine old buildings in the 1960s, but a great deal is as he left it. The red castle still looks down on the Victorian Gothic station where Tom worked for years, and the Elizabethan shop-fronts, tiny alleys, the churches where the Owens worshipped and the houses where they lived are still there. He may already have known Housman's poem, 'The Welsh Marches':

High the vanes of Shrewsbury gleam
Islanded in Severn stream;
The bridges from the steepled crest
Cross the water east and west.

The flag of morn in conqueror's state
Enters at the English gate:
The vanquished eve, as night prevails,
Bleeds upon the road to Wales.

(*A Shropshire Lad*, xxviii)

To find Wilfred's home on the east side of town you cross the English Bridge, which has been widened and rebuilt since his day. (The smaller, older Welsh Bridge is unchanged). Pass the Wakeman School, overlooking the river, which stands on the site of the Technical School he attended, and the Norman abbey best known for its links with the mythical, medieval sleuth, Cadfael. Wilfred's name and that of his friend Stanley Webb are on a tablet near the west window, and a striking grey granite memorial was unveiled in the grounds in 1993. To the left of Abbey Foregate are what were then some quiet country roads. The Owens lived first at 1 Cleveland Place, Underdale Road, and then, from 1910, at 69 Monkmoor Road, known to them by the Indian name of Mahim. Wilfred had the attic overlooking the old racecourse and, in the distance, the Wrekin and Haughmond Hill. Much of his spare time was spent in this cramped room, writing and reading.

The countryside was almost on their doorstep. A favourite family walk was to Uffington, not the White Horse village but a hamlet just across the Severn with a picturesque mill, church and canal. On one of these walks, Wilfred noticed how the buttercup dust stuck to Harold's boots and coined the phrase "blessed with gold", eventually used in his poem 'Spring Offensive'.

Words were not his sole interest. He was fascinated by archaeology, and often cycled, with his brothers or Stanley, to the site of the ancient ruined city of Uriconium to prospect. Some of his finds ended up in the local museum. Although he did not buy *A*

15

Shropshire Lad until 1916, he could well have known Housman's poem about 'Uricon the city', with its theme that man is fated to repeat the past. With his cousins, Vera and Leslie Gunston, he formed an 'Astronomical, Geological and Botanical Society'. Leslie, two years younger, would become one of his closest friends.

Both teenage boys were great admirers of Keats. In 1911, visiting Teignmouth (the family had several cheap holidays, since Tom could get passes for the railway), Wilfred made a pilgrimage to the house where the poet had lived and wrote a quite accomplished sonnet in his honour. The older poet's influence on him has always been well-known but it was Harold who revealed that Wilfred feared he would die young, like Keats. No doubt he was haunted by the sonnet:

> When I have fears that I may cease to be
> Before my pen has gleaned my teeming brain ....

Harold says, "His obsession with time was extraordinary ... he was shaken with panic and fear that he would not have time, time, TIME" (JFO II, 263). It was not totally unreasonable in an age when large numbers of young people were carried off by TB or diphtheria; moreover, Susan was a hypochondriac who encouraged him to worry about his health. Chatterton, Byron, Shelley — these were other Romantic cult-figures who had not had a normal lifespan. He felt that precious time was slipping away and that he was not being allowed to develop his powers.

It made him savagely frustrated. Shrewsbury had a famous public school where he would have liked to go; instead he had to be content with four years at the Technical (where he made great progress in English and French). He dreamed of what he could have done with three years at Oxford, but that too was out of the question. In his late teens, looking at a newspaper office in Torquay, he said, "with terrible bitterness", "You know, Harold, if Mother and Father would only help me, I might be editor of that newspaper — no, no, not that one, a London paper — one day, but I must have help and I just can't get it" (JFO I, 188).

Leaving school in 1911, when he was eighteen, Wilfred spent a term as a pupil-teacher at the Wyle Cop School (now a private house), but was warned by his headmaster's wife that he would be most unhappy if he settled for it as a career. In view of the agonies D.H. Lawrence had endured a few years earlier this is probably true, although Wilfred was more patient with children. That autumn he travelled to London to take matriculation exams, and passed them, but did not do well enough to win a scholarship. The same thing happened later when he tried for an assisted place at Reading University. He never had the knack of coming top in exams.

But, in spite of Tom's scepticism, Susan insisted that he should not start work yet and needed more time to find his own way. After pulling strings with local clergymen, she got him introduced to the Reverend Herbert Wigan, vicar of Dunsden near Reading, who was prepared to take him on as an assistant and pupil. Of course the idea was that he should eventually make his career in the church. Wilfred was not keen, but, since university now seemed impossible, he agreed to try it. "He could only look upon any suggested occupation as a means to an end, and never as an end in itself", Harold writes. "He dimly realised the possession of a power within himself; he was also aware that this power was tightly locked and that only he himself could force and fashion the key which would unlock it for him" (JFO I, 184).

The young man who moved into Dunsden Vicarage in October 1911 was rather short (just under five foot six), very dark, and wore his hair unfashionably long to signal his artistic temperament. Professor Edith Morley, head of the English department at Reading, thought him "an unhappy adolescent, suffering badly from lack of understanding ... and in need of encouragement and praise" (Stallworthy, 75). It must have saddened her that such an obviously able boy was cut off from higher education.

Links with the university, where he attended English and botany classes, were one of the things that kept him going over the next year. Another was his friendship with Leslie Gunston, who lived nearby (the two boys read Swinburne together and showed each other their poems), and the village children, whom he loved. But the greater part of his time had to be spent assisting at services, teaching Sunday school, sitting through church meetings and visiting parishioners in their homes. Until then, he had not understood how the really poor lived. He read Ruskin and Shelley —

17

who, he found, had once lived near Dunsden and taken an interest in the poor — and his views moved quickly to the Left:

> I am increasingly liberalising and liberating my thought, spite of the Vicar's strong Conservatism.... From what I hear straight from the tight-pursed lips of wolfish ploughmen in their cottages, I might say there is material ready for another revolution. Perhaps men will *strike*, not with absence from work; but with arms at work. Am I for or against upheaval? I know not; I am not happy in these thoughts; yet they press upon me. (Letter 133)

The case of Violet, "a gentle little girl of five, fast sinking under Consumption", particularly upset him. "The Father is perennially out of work, and the Mother I fancy half-starving for the sake of four children" (Letter 129). Later he found out what was really wrong with Violet, "debility due to malnutrition" (Letter 141).

These and other comments show that Wilfred's strong humanitarianism did not suddenly spring into existence during the war; it had always been part of his nature. A year after coming to Dunsden he assisted at the funeral of a woman and her four-year-old daughter, apparently killed in an accident, which inspired his finest poem yet:

> Deep under turfy grass and heavy clay
> They laid her bruised body, and the child.
> Poor victims of a swift mischance were they,
> Adown Death's trapdoor suddenly beguiled.
> I, weeping not, as others, but heart-wild,
> Affirmed to Heaven that even Love's fierce flame
> Must fail beneath the chill of this cold shame.
>
> So I rebelled, scorning and mocking such
> As had the ignorant callousness to wed
> On altar steps long frozen by the touch
> Of stretcher after stretcher of our dead.
> Love's blindness is too terrible, I said....

The feeling is the same as in 'Greater Love', written five or six years later; what really affects the poet, and seems ultimately most meaningful, is not love but death. He must also have felt, as he would in the war years, that he was leading a double life. Although this poem concludes that after all it is worth having children, because they are valuable in themselves, there is no trace of Christian hope in it.

Indeed by this time he was sure that Dunsden was a dead end. He was "flogging himself", in Harold's words, writing poetry late at night after long hours of parish work, suffering bad dreams and teenage sexual agonies and feeling hopelessly cut off from the world of literature. He could only cheer himself up by occasional breaks from the vicarage, such as an excursion to London where he saw, and wrote an awed poem about, a lock of Keats' hair. He commented wryly that it was foolish to be in love with a dead poet, instead of a live woman. The Vicar and his assistant, Clyde Black, kept pressing him to make a personal commitment to Christ. Something had to give.

At Christmas 1912, Black gave him a book on Elizabeth Barrett Browning, to which I shall return. In January 1913 there was a great scene and he wrote an emotional letter home which appears to be saying that he had "discovered" (seen through?) the Vicar "something over a year ago". "Murder will out", he concluded, "and I have murdered my false creed.... Escape from this hotbed of religion I now long for more than I could ever have conceived" (Letter 172). Soon afterwards he came home and collapsed with a chest illness which may have been partly psychosomatic. He was now sure that he had ceased to be an orthodox Christian, and the anti-clericalism in his later poems may well be connected with the Reverend Mr Wigan.

All kinds of depressing thoughts would have gone through his head as he lay in his attic with its view of the wintry hills, being nursed by Susan. He had wasted over a year, and got no further on. Harold left in March, to join the Merchant Service, and when he returned some months later, having been seriously ill in Calcutta, he got no sympathy from Wilfred:

> "Why must you come back with your talk of Italy and India, places I have never seen — and, worse still, sow seeds of discontent in me.... Am I — I — to be the one to moulder in a rustic village, while you, bull-like in your bovine stupidity, career unobservantly all over the world? Answer

me, wretched boy, answer me." (JFO II, 204)

His thoughts turned more and more to France. He had spent two holidays there with his father, and spoke the language well. "If I have got to live in poverty and extreme discomfort, at least I would prefer to do it in a civilised country" (JFO II, 196). In the end he was offered a post with a tiny salary, teaching English at the Berlitz School of Languages, Bordeaux. He left home with high hopes in September 1913.

From this time on his letters become distinctly more cheerful. He was kept hard at work — once saying that he only had an hour to himself each day — but any leisure he got here was much more precious than in Shrewsbury. He celebrated his twenty-first birthday in March 1914, grew a moustache (which made him look slightly French) and enjoyed some cautious flirtations with Frenchwomen. There was Henriette, a girl with "marvellous eyes" who made a strong impression, and the town clerk's curlyheaded daughter whom, he confided in Mary, he had kissed. Also Madame Léger, a married pupil who invited him to spend the summer of 1914 in the Pyrenees with her family, made it plain that she found him very attractive indeed.

Many critics believe that Wilfred was a repressed homosexual (or perhaps not repressed in the last year of his life). This seems possible, but not certain; while some poems ('Maundy Thursday') and passages in his letters could be interpreted that way there are others which suggest a deep attraction to the opposite sex:

> Now he will never feel again how slim
> Girls' waists are, or how warm their subtle hands.
> ('Disabled')

The rumour was started by Robert Graves who described him as "an idealistic homosexual" in a cancelled passage of *Goodbye to All That* (1929). Harold did not believe this and quotes him saying of young women, at their last meeting:

> "I like them very much ... but ... I must not let myself think about them. If I do they will come between me and my work and *nothing, nothing* must do that. I have so little time left".
> (JFO III, 163).

Against this it has been argued that Graves was unreliable, or —
alternatively — that Wilfred would not have told his younger
brother everything. What is certain is that he was celibate for most
of his life, perhaps all. Idealism kept him from taking the opportunities for casual sex on offer in Bordeaux; on the other hand, he
was too emotionally involved with Susan to form a serious relationship with a 'nice' girl. He would also have known that marriage was out of the question for many years. He could barely
support himself.

His attitude to women will be studied in later chapters. Meanwhile, it is not a bad idea for our own permissive age to remember
that a bookish young person may talk, write and dream of sex yet
carefully stay clear of any real involvement. Wilfred's energies,
from his early teens, went into literature and not much was left
over. My own guess is that if he had lived longer, he might have
gone either way. Or he might even have continued celibate; as he
"stormed" at Harold in 1914, "I don't want to be a man. I want to
be a poet. I want to write. I must write" (JFO III, 61).

"Amazing pleasure", was how Wilfred summed up his summer
at Bagnères-de-Bigorre with the Léger family, before and after war
broke out. In a poem written later, he spoke of

> A maid
> Laughing the love-laugh with me; proud of looks.
> The heat
> Throbbing between the upland and the peak.
> Her heart
> Quivering with passion to my pressed cheek.
> ('From my Diary, July 1914').

Who knows how much of this is imagination? His hosts were an
affluent and cultured family. M. Alfred Léger was an actor-man-
ager, who claimed to have known Mrs Browning in his youth.
Since she died in 1861, he cannot have been much below sixty. His
wife, whose first name has not come down to us, was thirty-one.
They had a precocious eleven-year-old daughter, Nénette, who
'wrote', and with whom Wilfred became great friends.

The elegant Madame Léger, who ran an interior decoration
business, soon told him that she was not in love with her husband.

She was going without her family to Canada (hence the English lessons) and suggested that Wilfred should come too. The flirtation went on against a background of brilliant weather and the outbreak of war in early August. As described in the preface, he climbed the Pyrenees on nights when there was a full moon and looked down into the still peaceful land of Spain. He could hardly help referring to the great upheaval in his letters, but at this time and for the next year they are surprisingly laid-back. One, written to his mother at the end of the month, could be considered callous:

> The war affects me less than it ought ... I feel my own life all the more precious and more dear in the presence of this deflowering of Europe. While it is true that the guns will effect a little useful weeding, I am furious with chagrin to think that the Minds which were to have excelled the civilisation of ten thousand years, are being annihilated — and bodies, the product of aeons of Natural Selection, melted down to pay for political statues. I regret the mortality of the English regulars less than that of the French, Belgian, or even Russian or German armies: because the former are all Tommy Atkins, poor fellows, while the continental armies are inclusive of the finest brains and temperaments of the land. (Letter 285)

For him the great event of August 1914 was his meeting with the elderly poet Laurent Tailhade, who was introduced to him by the Legers and with whom he had long literary conversations. The Frenchman, an anarchist and poet of the 'decadent' school, had in the past written pamphlets urging conscripts to refuse to serve. He was very friendly to Wilfred (who, however, was startled when Tailhade "slobbered" over him) and gave him a book of his verse.

Instead of rushing home to enlist, he moved back to Bordeaux, taking pupils, going to free courses and possibly educating himself in French poetry, although he told his mother that he had been reading hardly any verse. It was May before he crossed the channel, then returned to Bordeaux and was back in Shrewsbury by September. He had talked for some time about the possibility of enlisting but it was not until 21 October 1915, fourteen months after the war had started, that he finally joined the romantically-named Artists' Rifles, from which he would be commissioned into the Manchester Regiment the following year.

As has been said, Wilfred took a detached attitude to the war at first, and he wrote little about his reasons for enlisting. Probably the main one was that "it's not very natural for most people to peel themselves away from their generation", as a conscientious objector in a later war said. Edward Thomas, Isaac Rosenberg and Charles Sorley all had their doubts about the official line, yet all joined the army without compulsion. At the time Wilfred certainly believed that the Allied cause was just, having referred to "the foul tornado, centred at Berlin" in his sonnet '1914'; what was less clear to him was whether he need get involved personally.

On returning to England he came up against a tremendously powerful propaganda machine; young men not in khaki were regarded as cowards and sometimes given a white feather. (One of them, incidentally, was my grandfather, who later joined the Royal Welsh Fusiliers and was gassed). Harold says that "being branded with lack of courage, and the ostracism which would follow — this prospect and all its consequences he found appalling, and much more frightening than the horrid thought of army discipline" (JFO, II, 120). With his deep sense of responsibility and the ideals of self-sacrifice which had been instilled in him, he began to feel he could not stay aloof for ever. He wrote to his mother, attempting to show his independence of mind, "I don't want the bore of training, I don't want to wear khaki; nor yet to save my honour before inquisitive grandchildren fifty years hence. But I *now do* most *intensely want to fight* "(Letter 357).

He enjoyed his first weeks of training in London, where he visited the Poetry Bookshop and discussed his work with the proprietor, Harold Monro. Various military camps (including one at his birthplace, Oswestry) were less pleasant, and the bullying and crude language of the NCOs must have been a shock. Rosenberg was treated brutally during his training. Wilfred apparently did better, but, when Harold visited him in the early days, he thought he looked out of place. Then and later, he was prepared to strain every nerve to do what the Army wanted; inwardly, though, he was not reconciled:

"What does Keats have to teach me of rifle and machinegun drill, how will my pass in Botany teach me to lunge a bayonet, how will Shelley show me how to hate or any poet teach me the trajectory of the bullet?" (JFO III, 144)

Yet the story of the next year is of how this essentially gentle young man was turned into an efficient killing machine. He was recommended for a commission, not surprisingly, for the traditional officer class had already been killed off and there was a great shortage of intelligent men. When Harold next met him he saw a new and different Wilfred. His hair was cut short in a "frightful military crop" and he had obviously bent all his energy on becoming a model officer:

> "You know, Harold, if I have got to be a soldier, I must be a good one, anything else is unthinkable. I cannot alter myself inside nor yet conform but at least without any self-questioning I can change outside, if that is what is wanted. D'you remember us running along the High Street with my coat all buttoned up wrong? I can't do that sort of thing now ... outwardly I will conform ... my inward force will be the greater for it" (JFO III, 155).

He crossed the channel in the last days of 1916 and arrived at Beaumont Hamel, on the Somme — a very different France from the one where he had been so happy. Its blasted, treeless landscape has been made familiar to us by paintings and photographs; what these cannot convey is the smell ("its odour is the breath of cancer") and the constant thunder of guns. Wilfred had to wear "ear-defenders" to get used to this. He had also been unprepared for the mud and the coldest winter for thirty years. The land was under snow, "pock-marked ... like the face of the moon chaotic, crater-ridden, uninhabitable" (Letter 481). His platoon marched to the front through "an octopus of sucking clay" to hold a dug-out in the middle of No Man's Land. The letter he wrote home, after being relieved, shows his shock:

> I can see no excuse for deceiving you about these last 4 days. I have suffered seventh hell.
> I have not been at the front.
> I have been in front of it.... My dug-out held 25 men tight packed. Water filled it to a depth of 1 or 2 feet, leaving say

4 feet of air.... The Germans knew we were staying there
and decided we shouldn't.
Those fifty hours were the agony of my happy life.
Every ten minutes on Sunday afternoon seemed an
hour.
I nearly broke down and let myself drown in the water
that was now slowly rising over my knees. (Letter 480)

Probably the one thing that stopped him breaking down was the
knowledge that he was responsible for over forty men (there were
several more in another dug-out which Wilfred eventually visited,
crawling slowly across No Man's Land under fire from his own
side). A great deal has been written, some of it very sentimental,
about the relationship between officers — educated men like
Wilfred — and troops. In almost every case it is the officers' words
that have come down to us; Isaac Rosenberg and Ivor Gurney are
among the very few Other Ranks to give their point of view.
Wilfred's early experience of looking after the younger children,
and as a parish worker, had prepared him for being a father-figure
to the uneducated men under his command. There were other
aspects of this relationship, to be explored later, but at least he
would never again write patronisingly about Tommy as he had
done in August 1914. All agree that he was a conscientious and
well-liked officer.

The experience was one he would turn into poetry, but not yet.
'The Sentry', completed a year and a half later, probably gives a
close description of what happened:

We'd found an old Boche dug-out, and he knew,
And gave us hell; for shell on frantic shell
Lit full on top, but never quite burst through.
Rain, guttering down in waterfalls of slime,
Kept slush waist-high and rising hour by hour,
And choked the steps too thick with clay to climb.
What murk of air remained stank old, and sour
With fumes from whizz-bangs, and the smell of men
Who'd lived there years, and left their curse in the den,
If not their corpses ....
                      There we herded from the blast
Of whizz-bangs; but one found our door at last, —
Buffeting eyes and breath, snuffing the candles,

And thud! flump! thud! down the steep steps came
    thumping
And sploshing in the flood, deluging muck,
The sentry's body; then his rifle, handles
Of old Boche bombs, and mud in ruck on ruck.
We dredged it up, for dead, until he whined,
'O sir — my eyes, — I'm blind, — I'm blind, — I'm blind'.
Coaxing, I held a flame against his lids
And said if he could see the least blurred light
He was not blind; in time they'd get all right.
'I can't', he sobbed. Eyeballs, huge-bulged like squids',
Watch my dreams still, — yet I forgot him there
In posting Next for duty, and sending a scout
To beg a stretcher somewhere, and flound'ring about
To other posts under the shrieking air.

Those other wretches, how they bled and spewed,
And one who would have drowned himself for good, —
I try not to remember these things now.
Let Dread hark back for one word only: how,
Half-listening to that sentry's moans and jumps,
And the wild chattering of his shivered teeth,
Renewed most horribly whenever crumps
Pummelled the roof and slogged the air beneath, —
Through the dense din, I say, we heard him shout
'I see your lights!' — But ours had long gone out.

The "one who would have drowned himself for good" is Wilfred. The smell, the fearsome noise, the horror of seeing a man blinded (for it is clear that he will not recover) would never leave him. He had grown up with the vision of hell as a place of darkness and torment, now; he believed, he had experienced the reality. His overpowering feeling was that he had been lied to; that nobody had told him war was like this.

There were further horrors. He got his first whiff of 'GAS'; later the same January, his platoon "had to lie in the snow under the deadly wind. By day it was impossible to stand up or even crawl about". (This is the basis of 'Exposure'). One man died of cold. They were "marooned on a frozen desert ... not a blade of grass, not an insect" (Letter 482).

Next month he was out of action, and his letters grew more

cheerful. But in March, while going up the line with a digging party, he fell into a cellar and was concussed; this happened in pitch dark and he was apparently trapped for several hours. Pronounced fit, he went back into action outside St Quentin and wrote later that "going over the top" was like falling off a precipice. "There was an extraordinary exultation in the act of slowly walking forward, showing ourselves openly" (Letter 510). But after that it was purely passive suffering. For twelve days he sheltered in a railway cutting, "in a hole just big enough to lie in" (Letter 505), while opposite the body of another second lieutenant was blown all over the place by the shells. He wrote afterwards that what had really upset him was the sight of the unburied dead. During this time a shell blew him into the air, and it was this experience which led, some days later, to his being found unfit to command troops.

A mystery surrounds what happened to Wilfred at this time, partly because he may not have remembered everything and partly because he, his family and friends may well have wished to hush it up. He was not hurt, except for the bump on his head, and his letters are quite coherent, but he was shaky, stammering and had horrifying dreams. The doctor diagnosed neurasthenia and it was serious enough to keep him out of action for over a year. According to Graves, who met him some months later, "it preyed on his mind that he had been unjustly accused of cowardice by his commanding officer" (*Goodbye to All That*, Chapter 24).

Wilfred would say, in one of his most haunting lines of poetry:

Foreheads of men have bled where no wounds were

and it is interesting that many of the soldiers executed for cowardice or desertion had been shell-shocked and were sent back into action before they were fit. He was lucky to get more understanding treatment. A doctor who had wide experience of the western front later wrote:

The most likely type of man for 'shell-shock' is the brooding, introspective, self-analysing man ... whose imagination added the terrors of the future to those of the present. (quoted Anthony Babington, *For the Sake of Example* [1983], 266).

Edward Thomas had been killed (in the same month, April 1917) by the blast of a shell which did no other damage to his body. On Wilfred, the effect was less obvious. Contemporary accounts suggest that the C.O. did indeed call him a coward; according to Charles Scott Moncrieff he was sent home "in a state which hinted at a loss of morale under shell-fire". These words would eventually influence his decision to go back.

He was shipped home to England and appeared before a medical board which reported "there is little abnormality to be observed but he seems to be of a highly-strung temperament" (Stallworthy 187). He was then sent to Craiglockhart War Hospital, an imposing Victorian mansion outside Edinburgh, now used for the care of shell-shocked officers (and today part of Napier University). He would stay there for the next four months, carrying invisible wounds.

Wilfred's fellow-patients at Craiglockhart are described in his poem, 'Mental Cases', and the worst of them were in a pitiable state. During the day the hospital was full of cheerful activity, but at night, as Siegfried Sassoon would find, things changed:

> the place was full of men whose slumbers were morbid and terrifying — men muttering uneasily or suddenly crying out in their sleep.... In the daytime, sitting in a sunny room, a man could discuss his psycho-neurotic symptoms with his doctor.... But by night each man was back in his doomed sector of a horror-stricken front line where the panic and stampede of some ghastly experience was re-enacted among the livid faces of the dead. No doctor could save him then. (*Sherston's Progress* [1936], Part 1, Chapter 5).

Two men were responsible for steering Wilfred back to normality. One was Sassoon, as the world knows; the other was his doctor, Arthur Brock. A dedicated physician, interested in many things beyond his job, Brock believed that modern man had lost touch with nature and that neurosis was the inevitable result. "If civilisation is to be saved from perishing, it must rapidly, like Antaeus, regain its footing upon Mother Earth" DH 92).

Wilfred shared his doctor's interest in natural history, and the Greek myth of Antaeus, the giant who drew his strength from the earth and was killed by being lifted off it, made a lot of sense to him. As part of his therapy he wrote a long poem on this subject, showing two giants locked in deadly combat:

> Men say their fettered fury tightened hour by hour,
> Until the veins rose tubrous on their brows
> And froth flew thickly-shivered from both beards.
>
> ('The Wrestlers')

One of them suggests a truce but the other wants total victory. It sounds like a parable of the western front.

Brock also helped him to found the Craiglockhart Field Club, to study the ecology of the Pentlands region. He was soon reading and lecturing on plants and moss, which must have been soothing after the ruined landscape round Beaumont Hamel, "not a blade of grass, not an insect". He went hill-walking, became editor of the hospital magazine *The Hydra*, and met some Edinburgh families including the Newboults, whose son Arthur is the small boy in the famous photograph. He visited the slums with his new friends and began to learn German. Later he would teach boys at a local school about English literature and "the international idea" (Letter 550).

Siegfried Sassoon arrived at Craiglockhart several weeks later. A tall, striking-looking man, six years older than Wilfred, he had grown up with privileges the latter could only dream of. Although his father's family were of Middle Eastern Jewish origin, he had been brought up as an upper-class Englishman, going to Marlborough and then Cambridge, which he left without taking a degree. He then lived at home in Kent on his private income, went hunting, and published several slim volumes of poetry at his own expense. This had made him friends in the literary world and one of his early war poems, 'To Victory', had appeared in *The Times*. He had fought with great courage and won the Military Cross (which he later threw in the Mersey), but during sick leave in 1917 he had turned against the war. After discussions with the editor of *The Nation*, a liberal weekly, and with Bertrand Russell, he wrote an open letter to his commanding officer:

> I am making this statement as an act of wilful defiance of

military authority, because I believe that the war is being deliberately prolonged by those who have the power to end it.

I am a soldier, convinced that I am acting on behalf of soldiers. I believe that this war, upon which I entered as a war of defence and liberation, has now become a war of aggression and conquest. I believe that the purposes for which I and my fellow-soldiers entered upon this war should have been so clearly stated as to have made it impossible to change them, and that, had this been done, the objects which actuated us would now be attainable by negotiation.

I have seen and endured the sufferings of the troops, and I can no longer be a party to prolong these sufferings for ends which I believe to be evil and unjust.

I am not protesting against the conduct of the war, but against the political errors and insincerities for which the fighting men are being sacrificed.

On behalf of those who are suffering now I make this protest against the deception which is being practised on them; also I believe that I may help to destroy the callous complacency with which the majority of those at home regard the continuance of agonies which they do not share, and which they have not sufficient imagination to realise.

This statement was printed in several newspapers and discussed in the House of Commons. His friends, even those who disapproved of the war, were shocked, for apparently no one had ever yet done what Sassoon had and it seemed certain that he would be court-martialled and severely punished. Robert Graves, a poet in the same regiment who was also home on sick leave, did everything he could to defuse the situation. He believed that Siegfried's protest would do no good and blamed the pacifists, who had in fact warned him to think seriously about what he was doing. "I felt that, not being soldiers, they could not understand what it cost Siegfried emotionally" (*Goodbye to All That*, Chapter 24). Sassoon had started a debate which is still rolling. Meanwhile it was announced that he had had a nervous breakdown and, convinced that he could do no more, he allowed himself to be sent to Craiglockhart. His book, *The Old Huntsman*, dedicated to Hardy and containing several war poems, had been published that spring.

Had it not been for Wilfred (who had still written none of his best work) Sassoon would undoubtedly be remembered as the great poet of the First World War. The younger man read his book with enormous excitement, writing home, "Nothing like his trench life sketches has ever been written or ever will be written" (Letter 540). After long hesitations, he nerved himself to knock on Sassoon's door and asked him to autograph some copies. It was the most significant meeting of his life.

For Siegfried, the relationship was less important. There was not such a wide gulf between two young officers as there was between either one of them and 'the men', but his first impression was of a rather ordinary young man, probably speaking with a Shropshire accent and certainly unsophisticated compared to himself. But he welcomed the chance to discuss poetry and the war, and allowed Wilfred to show him his own work. He noticed the "velvety quality" of his voice, and that "his thick dark hair was already touched with white above the ears". Later he realised that

> in a young man of twenty-four his selflessness was extra-
> ordinary. The clue to his poetic genius was sympathy, not
> only in his detached outlook upon humanity but in all his
> actions and responses towards individuals. I can remember
> nothing in my observations of his character which showed
> any sign of egotism or desire for self-advancement (SJ 61)

In Wilfred's lifetime, though, Sassoon's attitude remained that of a patron. "I am sure he will be a very good poet some day, and he is a very loveable creature" (Siegfried Sassoon, *Diaries 1915-1918* [1983], 196).

For Wilfred, Sassoon had not only crystallised his attitude to the war — urging him to read *The Nation*, Wells and Russell — but had also shown him how to express anger and sorrow in poetry. He could now apply his formidable technique to his own experiences:

> ...you have *fixed* my Life, however short. You did not light me:
> I was always a mad comet; but you have fixed me. I spun
> round you a satellite for a month, but I shall swing out soon,
> a dark star in the orbit where you will blaze. (Letter 557)

In Harold's phrase, he had for years been "tunnelling alone" (JFO II, 37), unsure where all his studying and writing would lead him; now, like Keats, he would crowd his great poems into little more than a year. He began work immediately on 'The Dead-Beat', a poem in Sassoon's 'unheroic' style which was not finalised for some time. Two months later, when he showed him 'Anthem for Doomed Youth' which they revised together, it "dawned on" Sassoon "that my little friend was much more than the promising minor poet I had hitherto adjudged him to be" (SJ, 59). He introduced him to Graves, who was also impressed, and advised him to submit his work to national magazines.

Decision time was approaching as both young men neared the stage where they could be considered cured. Sassoon, and Wilfred after they became friends, had that little bit more freedom of manoeuvre than the common soldier and there was talk of safe jobs in England. That October Wilfred wrote, "I feel that I must first get some reputation of gallantry before I could successfully and usefully declare my principles" (Letter 550), but he would not finally make up his mind for some time.

Sassoon knew the authorities would not court-martial him and that he could, if he wished, sit out the war in Craiglockhart, playing golf while others were being killed. For a sensitive man with a deep feeling of solidarity for those left behind, it was a cruel dilemma. The poem 'Sick Leave' (originally it had the better title 'Death's Brotherhood'), written in the hospital and no doubt shown to Wilfred, reveals a process which was at work in both their minds:

> When I'm asleep, dreaming and lulled and warm, —
> They come, the homeless ones, the noiseless dead.
> While the dim charging breakers of the storm
> Bellow and drone and rumble overhead,
> Out of the gloom they gather about my bed.
> They whisper to my heart; their thoughts are mine.
> 'Why are you here with all your watches ended?
> From Ypres to Frise we sought you in the Line'.
> In bitter safety I awake, unfriended;
> And while the dawn begins with slashing rain
> I think of the Battalion in the mud.

'When are you going out to them again?
Are they not still your brothers through our blood?'

He eventually decided that he would go back and fight, but would not withdraw anything or pretend to have changed his mind. "While this agonising affair was in process", he wrote afterwards, Wilfred provided "gentle and intuitive support" (SJ 64).

During his last weeks at Craiglockhart, while spending each evening with Sassoon, Wilfred was continuing his German lessons with Frank Nicholson, the Librarian of Edinburgh University. He wrote afterwards that Wilfred "had brought with him from the Front a very keen realisation of the agony which the combatant nations, one and all, were enduring, and his sense of pity, which must have been strong in him by nature and had been intensified by his experiences, enabled him to regard Germany as a fellow-sufferer with the rest and made him wish, I think, to prepare himself for any future opportunities of holding intercourse with the Germans" (Blunden, 133). He also got the impression that Wilfred was making a collection of war photographs.

The lessons were interrupted at the end of October when Wilfred was examined and pronounced fit for light duties, then allowed three weeks leave. He left Edinburgh, where he had made so many friends, with a heavy heart, but Sassoon had already arranged to introduce him to people he knew on the literary and anti-war networks. There was also the hope that he might not, after all, be asked to fight again.

He now began at last to meet other writers regularly. Siegfried had put him in touch with Robert Ross, best known as Oscar Wilde's friend, an art dealer and critic who did an extraordinary amount to help young writers get into print. Many other poets spoke warmly of his kindness. According to Osbert Sitwell it was he (not Wilfred) who had some horrifying war photographs and would show them to the noisier type of patriot saying "then these might interest you". Ross gave him lunch in the Reform Club where he found himself talking to Arnold Bennett and H.G. Wells. He made a good impression, partly through his poetry, which was beginning to circulate in manuscript, and partly through his modest and pleasant manners.

Ever since he came back from the front, he would have felt, like

Sassoon and many others, that it was impossible to make people at home understand what it was like. "England looked strange to us returned soldiers", wrote Graves. "We could not understand the war-madness that ran wild everywhere.... The civilians talked a foreign language, and it was newspaper language. I found serious conversation with my parents all but impossible" (*Goodbye to All That*, Chapter 21). Perhaps there is some exaggeration, but it is true that in the war years Britain became more like a totalitarian state than at any time before or since. D.H. Lawrence, who escaped conscription through his frail health, would write:

> From 1916 to 1919 a wave of criminal lust rose and possessed England, there was a reign of terror, under a set of indecent bullies like Bottomley of *John Bull* and other bottom-dog members of the House of Commons.... The torture was steadily applied, during those years after Asquith fell, to break the independent soul in any man who would not hunt with the criminal mob.... During the crucial years of the war, the people chose, and chose Bottomleyism. Bottom enough. (*Kangaroo*, Chapter 12.)

John Bull was a jingo paper, much read by the troops; Horatio Bottomley (1860-1933), its editor, was a super-patriot later to be exposed as a swindler on a grand scale. Wilfred, coming back from a short visit to Leslie Gunston near Winchester, found himself sharing a railway carriage with the great man. He did not speak to him, but looked out of the window and "could almost see the dead lying about in the hollows of the downs" (Letter 561). This inspired his poem 'Asleep'.

At the end of November he reported to Scarborough, as ordered, and found himself billeted at the Clarence Gardens (now Clifton) Hotel. It was full of officers and Wilfred's job was to look after all domestic arrangements as assistant to the Mess President, Lieutenant Priestley. Roland Bate, a former theological student who saw him going about his work, wrote:

> He led a life of extreme detachment from his fellow men. He moved about like Priestley's shadow; I do not recollect him ever talking to me or any other subaltern and I never caught from him a glimpse of a smile.... The Colonel at

> Scarborough was a 'dug-out' regular soldier too old for active service. He had lost two sons, killed in the war, and he had no understanding of or sympathy with 'shell-shock' or neurasthenia. He had a special 'down' on Owen, who was on light duty and excused all parades, and seemed bent on pushing him back to France. (W. Roland Bate, 'Sixty years Ago', *Blackwood's Magazine*, November 1975).

It will be seen that Wilfred made quite different impressions in literary and military circles. If he was nervous and withdrawn at this time, small wonder; the colonel's attitude could only have increased his heavy feelings of guilt. He sheltered behind Priestley, a genial man, and went with him to the local antique shops. Otherwise he made few friends, for he was intensely conscious that he had only about half an hour a day to himself. He was given a turret room, overlooking the North Bay, and isolated himself there in the evenings to read and write. He would remain in Scarborough for the next three months.

A few days after he arrived, on 29 November 1917, the *Daily Telegraph* published a famous letter from Lord Lansdowne. The aged statesman, who had lost a son at the front, argued, like Sassoon, that the allies should state their war aims and explore the possibility of a negotiated peace:

> we are slowly but surely killing off the best of the male population of these islands ... the responsibility of those who needlessly prolong such a war is not less than those who needlessly provoke it.

This modest suggestion was greeted by a storm of outrage. No comment from Wilfred survives, but it must have confirmed his belief that the world had gone mad. Throughout the autumn and winter, though, more people began cautiously to talk about peace.

He read Barbusse's war novel, *Le Feu*, wrote and revised poems, spent some pleasant hours bargaining for pieces of furniture, with the idea of moving out of home after the war. In December Sassoon went back to active service, feeling like a condemned man. On New Year's Eve Wilfred wrote to his mother in words which have become famous, and which sum up graphically his life so far:

Bouts of awful labour at Shrewsbury & Bordeaux; bouts of amazing pleasure in the Pyrenees, and play at Craiglock-hart; bouts of religion at Dunsden; bouts of horrible danger on the Somme; bouts of poetry always; of your affection always; of sympathy for the oppressed always.

I go out of this year a Poet, my dear Mother, as which I did not enter it. I am held peer by the Georgians; I am a poet's poet.

I am started. The tugs have left me; I feel the great swelling of the open sea taking my galleon. (Letter 578)

On 12 January 1918 there was an appalling pit disaster at Hal-merend, and two weeks later *The Nation* published his poem 'Miners'. This was the first time he had appeared in a national magazine (he had had a couple of poems in the hospital's *Hydra*), and must have been one of the best moments of his life. *The Nation*, which had had censorship problems throughout the war and was banned overseas, was one of the few voices to have supported Lansdowne. By sending his work there, Wilfred was associating himself with its political stand.

Just before 'Miners' came out, he visited London for Robert Graves' wedding and found that people were already referring to him as 'Owen the poet'. Here he met Charles Scott Moncrieff, a poet and translator who had been wounded in France and was now working at the War Office. After Wilfred's death he would anger his family and friends by repeating the 'cowardice' story, and it is also known that he became infatuated with him, and wrote him some pseudo-Shakespearean sonnets, over the next few months. Wilfred, though, did not respond as he would have liked.

Philip Larkin — following other critics — wrote "it cannot be ignored that in the last year of his life he was moving in homosexual society" (*Required Writing*, [1983], 235). The last year of Wilfred's life was spent chiefly in military establishments in Ripon and Scarborough, whence he wrote to Leslie at the end of 1917 about an encounter with some chorus girls with "adorable slender bare legs" (Letter 577). Such leave as he got had to be spent partly at home, although he was gently making it clear to Susan that he could not give her all his free time. During 1918 he managed a few weekends in London and crammed as much as possible into them, but he went there for precious intellectual contacts, not orgies. He guarded his spare time, keeping aloof from the bridge-playing officers in camp who did not know he wrote poetry. Those whose friendship he sought were people who shared his literary interests and/or his opposition to the war.

Scott Moncrieff was pro-war, but he was very interested in Wilfred's use of half-rhyme. They talked for some hours about poetry. Later it occurred to him that he could do Wilfred a good turn by finding him a safe job.

In March he was transferred from Scarborough to an army camp outside Ripon where he found himself sharing a hut with thirteen officers. Desperate for a quiet place to work, he hired an attic five minutes' walk away, in a cottage in Borrage Lane which is still standing. He walked there daily, after finishing exercises in mid-afternoon, and spent the evenings drafting new poems and polishing old ones. It was pleasant wooded countryside with a "happy little stream", the River Skell, and lesser celandines coming into flower. Children played war games in the lane outside.

On 21 March, three days after his twenty-fifth birthday, the Germans launched their last great offensive of the war. Wilfred felt numb as he read how the places he had fought over last spring had been reoccupied; the good weather was spoiled for him by "the vision of the lands about St Quentin crawling with wounded" (Letter 608). The British casualties were horrifying; his old Shrewsbury friend, Stanley Webb, was killed, as was a little-known poet, Isaac Rosenberg. He worried about his beloved youngest brother, Colin, who was coming up to eighteen. The movement for a negotiated peace suffered a fatal blow:

> Because I perfectly foresaw these days, it was that I said it would have been better to make peace in 1916. Or even last Autumn. It certainly is 'impossible' now. (Letter 607)

Wilfred was not yet considered quite well, but it was unlikely now that he would be allowed to stay in England. He also seems to have felt that it would not be right, and tried, through strenuous training, to get fit.

All he could do that spring, in the precious evening hours in his attic, was write. Several of the great poems — 'Insensibility', 'Strange Meeting', 'The Send-Off', 'Futility' — belong to this period. He had already told his mother that "I *bring on* what few war dreams I now have, entirely by *willingly* considering war of an evening" (Letter 592). "I try not to remember these things now", he would write in 'The Sentry', going back to the horror of his first weeks at the front. But it was necessary to remember, and to write them down, if his message was to get through. So he worked fiercely, in the spirit of Julian Grenfell's war hymn 'Into Battle', which he had read:

> If this be the last song you shall sing,
> Sing well, for you may not sing another.

In April he met Harold on a weekend leave in Shrewsbury (the younger brother expected to be sent on a dangerous mission) and they sat up all night talking and chain-smoking. Both were depressed, knowing that their chances of survival were slim. Next morning was gloomy, the Wrekin blotted out by mist:

> "Harold, was it for this we were born? You to go to your hungry seas and I to the shells and bullets of France, never to see each other again? Both to be killed or shattered, and my little Colin for the RFC? I can't believe it" (JFO III, 168).

Possibly Harold misquoted him after half a century, but the war was at its lowest point and it is easy to believe that Wilfred said something like this. Harold asked if he had made up his mind to get back to the front as soon as possible. Wilfred said yes

> "and I know I shall be killed. But it's the only place that I can make my protest from" (JFO III, 162).

But in May, when he snatched a weekend in London, his resolution wavered. Scott Moncrieff assured him that he could fix a home job instructing cadets. He also made it plain that he wanted more than a literary relationship, but Wilfred kept him at arm's length. A letter from France of 7 October 1918, which begins formally, "My dear Scott Moncrieff", shows that there were no especially warm feelings on his side.

He spent that weekend showing his new poems to Ross and meeting more writers including Osbert Sitwell, another young officer who had turned against the war, "a link of nonconformity that in those years bound together the disbelievers with almost the same force with which faith had knitted together the early Christians". Sitwell found him "the most diffident and sensitive of men", extremely quiet in the presence of Wells and Bennett:

> This silence, apart from being rooted in his natural modesty and good manners, was due, I think, to the immense esteem in which he held literature and those who practised the profession of author. His residence in France may have deepened this attitude of respect, and almost awe, which had in it nothing of the Englishman's casual approach to books. To him they were all-important, while poetry was the very crown of life. (*Noble Essences* [1950], Chapter 4)

Ross advised him to get his poems typed, and promised to help him publish a collection later that year. It did not happen, because Ross became ill soon afterwards and died just before the end of the war. But it was an intoxicating prospect for a young writer who had still had only one poem in print. Wilfred took it soberly and calmly. "Five years ago this would ... have turned my head — but nowadays my head turns only in shame away from these first flickers of the limelight. For I am old already for a poet, and so little is yet achieved" (Letter 622). He was simply grateful to have the respect of Sassoon and Graves, and anxious that anything he published should be worthy.

For this reason he spent his last weeks at Ripon planning a book of some thirty war poems, rejecting weaker early work and drafting a preface in which he hoped to strike at the public's conscience. At the beginning of June he was medically examined, pronounced fit and sent back to Scarborough. From this time the flow of great poems almost stops.

A letter to Susan explains why. "I cannot keep alive here long. Here one does not live at all. One eats, (badly) sleeps, (well) and works like a demented piece of clockwork" (Letter 627). He had a dirty tent with a cinder floor; he would not again get a room of his own. At the same time he was finally winning some recognition; 'Futility' and 'Hospital Barge at Cerisy' appeared in *The Nation*, and Osbert Sitwell and his sister Edith asked him to contribute to their magazine, *Wheels*. In the end they would be his first publishers.

But he now felt "incarcerated" (Letter 634), and probably had even less free time than the half hour per day he had snatched for poetry during his first stint at Scarborough. He was distressed by the sight of the thin, greenish-pale teenage conscripts who flooded into the barracks and whom he had to train. Possibly he began to think along the lines of Sassoon's reported words to Graves — "Our best place would be back in France away from the more shameful madness of home-service. There, our function would not be to kill Germans, though that might happen, but to make things easier for the men under our command. For them, the difference between being commanded by someone whom they could count as a friend — someone who protected them as much as he could from the grosser indignities of the military system — and having to study the whims of any petty tyrant in an officer's tunic, made all the difference in the world" (*Goodbye to All That*, Chapter 21).

Up to the end of June he was still talking about getting a home job, as often happened to officers who had broken down. Scott Moncrieff assumed he would have taken one had it been offered; in an article published after the war he wrote:

> He seemed secure for a moment until the Military Secretary's Department claimed that, having been sent home a year earlier in a state which hinted at a loss of morale under shell-fire, it was under shell-fire alone that he could be entrusted with the command of men. The case was put more briefly, but in words which do not look well in print. He was again placed on a draft. (*New Witness*, 10 December 1920).

This is probably true (although the files have disappeared), and it caused great embarrassment to Wilfred's family. But his letters, quoted below, prove that after long hesitations, he had made his own decision to go back. Since he no longer believed in the war — and would tell an officer he met in France that he thought the Allies were as bad as Germany — our generation may find it hard to understand why.

His options were limited. He had seen Sassoon's grand gesture collapse and realised that a single second lieutenant's protest would not alter the course of the war. And while Siegfried, with

his MC, could not possibly be accused of cowardice, that accusation had already been made against him and had "preyed on his
mind". In July he got news which, perhaps, tipped the balance.
Siegfried had been sent to Ireland, then Palestine and finally
France after the great German offensive. His book *Counter-Attack*,
full of bitter war poems which Wilfred had seen in manuscript,
was about to appear. Coming back from patrol, he had been shot
in the head by one of his own sergeants, and although the wound
was not serious his friends hoped he was now out of it for good.
Wilfred wrote to his mother, "Now must I throw my little candle
on his torch, and go out again" (Letter 641). Soon afterwards he
was able to tell her that it was settled.

There may have been another good reason for his decision, as
A. Alvarez wrote from the perspective of 1971 when young men
were refusing to fight in another war:

> He was going back to France because he had to do his
> duty as a soldier: since duty invariably means sacrifice,
> even the chance of the ultimate sacrifice must be accepted
> without fuss.
>
> But even more strongly, there is an anti-heroic force at
> work which corresponds to all those elements in his writing
> which went to make him one of the British forerunners of
> modernism; it corresponds, that is, to his poems' harsh,
> disabused version of the war and, technically, to their
> subtle, decisive use of half-rhymes which helped effectively
> to dispose of the chiming sweetness of much Georgian
> verse. It was this second force which impelled him to return
> to France not as 'an officer and a gentleman' but as a
> writer.... What drove him back, I think, had nothing to do
> with heroism and everything to do with poetry. The new
> powers he felt in himself seem to have been inextricably
> linked with the strange unprecedented vision he had had
> in France. (*The Savage God*, 201).

He walked on Scarborough sands, noticing the "stinking Leeds
and Bradford War-profiteers" (Letter 643) reading Bottomley's
paper. He also managed a quick trip to London where he visited
Sassoon in hospital, but did not tell him what he was about to do.
In his final days in England, he called at Shrewsbury to leave his
work in a safe place. The long hours of revision had paid off and

he now had several poems which he knew were good, though not all were completely finished or written out clearly. He had also started work on a preface to his hoped-for short book:

> This book is not about heroes. English Poetry is not yet fit to speak of them.
> Nor is it about deeds, or lands, nor anything about glory, honour, might, majesty, dominion, or power, except War.
> Above all I am not concerned with Poetry.
> My subject is War, and the pity of War.
> The Poetry is in the Pity.
> Yet these elegies are to this generation in no sense consolatory. They may be to the next. All a poet can do today is warn. That is why the true Poets must be truthful.
> (If I thought the letter of this book would last, I might have used proper names; but if the spirit of it survives — survives Prussia — my ambition and those names will have achieved fresher fields than Flanders....)

Wilfred crossed the channel on 31 August 1918. His second spell at the front would copy the sequence of events in 'Strange Meeting'.

He wrote to Siegfried some weeks later, "You said it would be a good thing for my poetry if I went back. That is my consolation for feeling a fool. This is what shells scream at me every time: Haven't you got the wits to keep out of this?" (Letter 660). During September, as he slowly moved towards the front line, he found time to do some work, revising 'The Sentry', 'Exposure', and 'Spring Offensive' and drafting a new poem, 'Smile, Smile, Smile', inspired by Clemenceau, the white-moustached French Premier whom he and Sitwell particularly loathed. The old man had been reported as saying that France and England must "keep on fighting victoriously until the moment when the enemy will understand there is no possible negotiation between crime and right". The war would go on to the bitter end.

His nerves were in a much better state than in 1917. Early in October they went into action and, probably to his own surprise, he distinguished himself. "It passed the limits of my Abhorrence. I lost all my earthly faculties, and fought like an angel" (Letter 662). A great many Germans, perhaps with no heart for more fighting, surrendered, but for another day they were stuck in a trench under heavy fire until relieved. A survivor, Lieutenant Foulkes, wrote, "This is where I admired his work — in leading his remnants, in the middle of the night, back to safety. I remember feeling how glad I was that it was not my job to know how to get out" (Blunden 37).

For this he was awarded the coveted Military Cross. He had wiped out the accusation of cowardice, at the price, perhaps, of smearing blood all over his soul. One version of the official account says:

> On the Company Commander becoming a casualty, he assumed command and showed fine leadership and resisted a heavy counter-attack. He personally captured an enemy machine gun in an isolated position and took a number of prisoners. Throughout he behaved most gallantly.

This agrees with Wilfred's own description, but there is another version which says:

> He personally manipulated a captured enemy M.G. from an isolated position and inflicted considerable losses on the enemy.

Whether officialdom got it wrong, or whether Wilfred could not bear to write about what he had done, there is quite a discrepancy. It is obvious that in the days after the attack he was trying not to think about it too deeply. "My senses are charred", he wrote to Sassoon. "I shall feel again as soon as I dare, but now I must not. I don't take the cigarette out of my mouth when I write Deceased over their letters. But one day I will write Deceased over many books" (Letter 664). Possibly it was after this that he added the last stanza to 'Spring Offensive'.

He was leading a schizophrenic life . Hardly anyone in the army knew he was a poet. He believed he had come back to help the men, yet he had written bitterly when he embarked, "I go among cattle to be a cattle-driver.... I am among the herds again, a Herdsman" (Letters 647 and 649). Late in October he "had the painful duty of collecting & goading along the stragglers" (Letter 669), and he also had to stand up in front of the troops to read a special order of 7 October, "All ranks are warned against the disturbing influence of dangerous peace talk.... Peace talk in any form is to cease in the Fourth Army".

Meanwhile, he was urging his mother to start some peace talk in England. Susan had good reason to do so, for all through October the end seemed in sight and both devoutly hoped that he would not have to fight again. Austria-Hungary had broken up, and the Germans had made peace overtures. It seemed that "the Rumble on the horizon may cease any hour. I'm listening now, but it still goes on, a gigantic carpet-beating" (Letter 668).

It was not only Wilfred Owen's life, and some thousands of others, that hung in the balance during these final weeks; it was also Europe's future. While some argued that the time had come to make peace, Clemenceau in France, Bottomley and the gutter press in England, demanded that Germany should surrender unconditionally and then be ground into the dust. This attitude would lead to the Treaty of Versailles and eventually the Second World War.

Wilfred was delighted to find that the exhausted men had turned against *John Bull*. He now thought there was a good chance that the war could be over by Christmas, and wrote that he was looking forward to being home by February, "with the keenness of frost and cold, blue sunlight", to climb the Wrekin and Haughmond Hill (Letter 670).

His hopes were dashed. At the end of October the Manchesters moved towards the Sambre and Oise canal, swollen with autumn rain, fringed by mutilated trees. In the early morning darkness of 4 November 1918, Wilfred and his companions approached the west bank with their floats and duckboards. They had the appalling task of getting across on a makeshift bridge while being fired on by machine-guns from the other side, and they had been told there could be no turning back. Casualties were very heavy, and the attack failed. The bridge was wrecked and not rebuilt.

Wilfred was last seen at the water's edge, giving a hand with the duckboards. Possibly he thought briefly of that other canal at Uffington, "fringed on either side with bulrushes ... sleeping with glassy stillness" (JFO I, 169); more likely he was wholly absorbed in encouraging the men when the machinegun hit him:

He 'fell' among planks awash,
hit and hit, smashed, gouged into
springing arrowhead shards under
the fire; by virtue of a crafty
self-deceit, by reason of a huge desire
for a virtuous reason to live, out of purest
nobility; among debris slithering
across Lethe, planks drifting waterlogged
and sideways, batted by each other,
nudged by shapes hunched underwater
like giants; he fell down among
matchsticks carrying the random and
slumped dead making a crossing.

(Judith Kazantzis, 'For example Owen')

While some accounts say he never left the bank, there is also a story that he was hit while on a raft. If so, his body was recovered from the water, like Shelley's, and eventually buried with the other dead in the military corner of Ors cemetery.

One week later, on 11 November, came the Armistice. It did not take effect until eleven o' clock, and several men were killed in the early hours of the day. In Shrewsbury, the church bells started ringing and for the next hour Tom and Susan must have allowed themselves to believe that their eldest son had survived. The telegram reached them at midday.

Harold was with his ship off Cape Town and found himself unable to rejoice or feel any sympathy with the cheering crowds on shore. A few days later he had a hallucination which convinced him that Wilfred was dead.

Sassoon spent the first months of peace celebrating and did not ask himself why his greatest admirer failed to write.

2: Poetry

"I don't think these shell-shocked war poems will move our grandchildren...."

The shots on the Sambre canal seven days before the end of the war changed the course of English literature. Many poets had already been killed (including, probably, some who were never heard of); Wilfred was the last and, as most people now think, the greatest. Had he lived he would certainly have become one of the leading literary men of his day. On the other hand, if he had not already made friends in the literary world, he could quite easily have been forgotten.

He had published only four poems in national magazines, and these not to everyone's taste. At the time, most people thought that the great poet of the war was Rupert Brooke. The Owen family in Shrewsbury did not have the sophistication or the literary contacts to get his papers into print. Most existed only as MSS, heavily corrected and presenting big editorial problems; even the famous Preface to his proposed book was incomplete.

It was the friends from the last year of his life who made the difference; poets who had survived the war and who felt a responsibility to those who had not. The 1919 issue of *Wheels* was dedicated to his memory and contained seven poems including 'Strange Meeting', which made the greatest impact then and since. Next year twenty-three poems came out in book form, introduced by Sassoon but edited by Edith Sitwell who had done all the real work, "disentangling the various versions of Wilfred Owen's war poems (sometimes almost indecipherable from the mud of the trenches smeared over them)" (*Taken Care Of,* [1965], 135). It was

received with respect; the half-rhymes being especially commented on. "The discovery of final assonances in place of rhyme",
Edmund Blunden wrote prophetically, "may mark a new age in
poetry" (*Athenaeum*, 10 December 1920).

Among his greatest admirers was John Middleton Murry who
wrote, in his review of the first collection:

> Wilfred Owen was the greatest poet of the war. There have
> been war-poets; but he was a poet of another kind. He was
> not a poet who seized upon the opportunity of war, but one
> whose being was saturated by a strange experience, who
> bowed himself to the horror of war until his soul was
> penetrated by it, and there was no mean or personal element
> remaining unsubdued in him.... Other poets — true poets
> some of them — have written of the war. Why are they less
> than he? For this single reason. The war was a terrible and
> unique experience in the history of mankind; its poetry had
> likewise to be unique and terrible; it had to record not the
> high hopes that animated English youth at the outset, but
> the slow destruction of that youth in the sequel; more than
> this, it had to record not what the war did to men's bodies
> and senses, but what it did to their souls. ('The Poet of the
> War', *Casebook*, 61).

'The poet of the war' — that is how Owen has been seen ever
since about 1920. Many have wondered what he would have
written next, or if he would have been stuck in a time-warp like
Sassoon, who survived him by fifty years but never shook off the
'war poet' label. There are some clues, in poems like 'Miners' and
'The Roads Also', and C. Day Lewis suggested that he might have
turned to "Catullan love poetry", but we shall never know. Only
a few people saw Wilfred's poems during his lifetime, so all later
readers were aware of the fact that he had been killed. That alone
gave the poems immense authority. Objectively, whether he died
in 1918 or 1968 could not effect their value; in practice, his early
death made him a prophet. Even those like Yeats and Newbolt
who disliked his work had to show some respect for him personally, for after all, he had done what a young man had to do.

But 'poet of the war' is a limiting phrase. After the first batch of
memorial volumes, everyone seemed to want to forget the last few

dreadful years, and the book had limited sales and brought in very small royalties for his family. Meanwhile the Modernist revolution (which had started before the war but been greatly speeded up by it) was spreading through the visual arts, music, the novel and verse. This was the beginning of a split, which has never been healed, between 'high' poetry, admired by critics but largely unread, and 'low' popular verse. Owen's technical experiments now seemed modest compared to the work of T.S. Eliot and the *vers libre* school. He was never forgotten, but his reputation was slow-growing; he did not appear in the *Dictionary of National Biography* as did the more acceptable Brooke and Grenfell (Wilfred finally made it into the Missing Persons' Supplement in his centenary year, 1993). He remained unpopular with those who took a conventional view of the war, and with his parents' generation. His accusation that the old men had sent the young ones to die seems to have struck a nerve, and was bitterly resented. A few young people in the 1920s, though, had already made a cult of him.

For a long time the war experience remained sealed in people's minds or ignored by those who had not been part of it. Poems could be printed or passed around while the fighting was still going on, but the great novels and memoirs of 1914-18 did not appear for another decade. As buried memories revived, with Sassoon and Graves among others publishing best-sellers, there was more interest in Owen. Arthur Bliss, who had been wounded and whose brother had been killed, included 'Spring Offensive' in his oratorio *Morning Heroes* (1929). In 1931 came a new edition of the poetry with a memoir by Edmund Blunden. The text was flawed, but it remained the only available version for over thirty years. Now that the war was seen as a hideous mistake and younger poets were moving to the Left, Owen's popularity increased. Auden, Isherwood and Spender all acknowledged his influence, and C. Day Lewis — who claimed "Hopkins, Owen and Eliot as our immediate ancestors" — paid a particularly warm tribute in 1934:

> Owen was not a technical revolutionary: his one innovation is the constant use of the alliterative assonance as an end rhyme — (mystery, mastery; killed, cold). But he was a true

revolutionary poet, opening up new fields of sensitiveness for his successors. If he had lived there is no knowing what his promise might have achieved; he would have found, active in different guises, the cant, the oppression, the sufferings and courage which had challenged his powers during the war. As it is, his unsentimental pity, his savage and sacred indignation are the best of our inheritance, and it is for his heirs to see that they are not wasted. (*A Hope for Poetry*, Chapter 3).

The older generation was not convinced. "I don't think these shell-shocked war poems will move our grandchildren greatly", the patriotic poet Sir Henry Newbolt predicted (*Casebook*, 65). W.B. Yeats excluded Owen from the *Oxford Book of Modern Verse* (1936) in what became a well-known literary scandal. Yeats is now thought to have come out of the argument badly, but he and other editors probably increased the time Owen spent in obscurity. He did not appear in some anthologies until the 1950s, his work was not taught in schools and most literary histories said little about the war poets, or treated them as a special case, outside the mainstream.

He remained popular with fellow-poets, less so with the general reader, until at least forty years after his death. The poets of the Second World War knew of him, and Dylan Thomas (a non-combatant) praised him highly in a radio talk of 1946:

> The voice of the poetry of Wilfred Owen speaks to us, down the revolving stages of thirty years, with terrible new significance and strength. We had not forgotten his poetry, but perhaps we had allowed ourselves to think of it as the voice of one particular time, one place, one war. Now, at the beginning of what, in the future, may never be known to historians as the 'atomic age' — for obvious reasons: there may be no historians — we can see, re-reading Owen, that he is a poet of all times, all places, and all wars. (*Quite Early One Morning*, 92)

Yet it would still take time. For many years after the Second World War, there were few serious studies of Owen and children were taught very little about the Great War and its poets. The verses quoted over and over again were Brooke's 'The Soldier',

Laurence Binyon's 'For the Fallen' and John McCrae's 'In Flanders Fields' with its vengeful message, "Take up our quarrel with the foe". It must be said too that many of Wilfred's generation were unwilling to hear him; D.S.R. Welland writes:

> In the 1950s, for example, when I included it as a matter of course in a Modern Literature syllabus for an Adult Education class some students withdrew in protest. Though unusual even then, the incident is not without significance. They were mostly older students who still remembered close relatives killed in the First World War and who felt that Owen's criticism of aspects of that war was in some way an insult to the memory of those relatives. Owen had himself recognised, again correctly, that 'these elegies are to this generation in no sense consolatory'; Rupert Brooke's poems still represented what my students wanted from a war poet. (Welland, 149)

In the 1960s things changed, for many possible reasons — that World War I could at last be seen in perspective, that it was a time when authority was being widely questioned, that we were seeing Vietnam on our screens. Young people who had not suffered like their fathers and grandfathers seemed particularly receptive to Owen's message:

> Ours was a gentle generation, pacific,
> In love with music, art and restaurants ....
> No friend of ours had ever been to war.
> (Douglas Dunn, 'December').

1960 saw the first full-length study, *Wilfred Owen* by D.S.R. Welland, and in the same year his poems finally appeared on the school English syllabus. Benjamin Britten in 1962 set nine poems to music in his *War Requiem*, which was performed for the first time in Coventry Cathedral to celebrate its reconstruction after being bombed in the Second World War:

> A musical statement of the first magnitude was called for ... Britten seized a final, momentous opportunity to make a public pronouncement of his passionately held pacifist convictions on the largest scale and in a way such as would

50

strike home to the largest possible number of listeners. "All a poet can do today is warn", Owen had said. *His* warnings had gone largely unheeded. Now, nearly fifty years later, and building on the foundations laid by Owen, Britten would warn again. (*War Requiem*, Decca booklet)

This caused sales of the poems to rise. In 1963 came a new edition, by C. Day Lewis, and in 1964 the fiftieth anniversary of the war brought renewed interest. Among the anthologies and critical studies featuring Owen and others were *Up the Line to Death* (1964), edited by Brian Gardner, and *Heroes' Twilight* (1965) by Bernard Bergonzi. There was also a flood of new information about Owen the man (till then, a shadowy figure) with Harold Owen's *Journey from Obscurity* (1963-5) and the *Collected Letters* (1967, edited by Harold Owen and John Bell). By the end of the decade it was possible to write, "Wilfred Owen has been found to haunt many a young reader unlike anybody else in adult writing" (Maurice Hussey, Introduction to *Poetry of the First World War*, 1969).

Since then, every aspect of his life and work has been studied intensively. The first biography was published in 1974 by Jon Stallworthy, who has also brought out a new, accurate edition, *Wilfred Owen: The Complete Poems and Fragments* (1983); other work of great value has been done by Dominic Hibberd and Sven Backman. Owen's influence has gone beyond English literature and into history, so that children studying the First World War now regularly read him and Sassoon. He has appeared in modern novels, plays and paintings, and seems likely to go on getting more and more popular. We have not rejected war, as he hoped, but most of us are at least conscious of what C. Day Lewis wrote in the introduction to his 1963 edition:

> It is Owen, I believe, whose poetry came home deepest to my own generation, so that we could never again think of war as anything but a vile, if necessary, evil.

It would have given him particular pleasure to know that the younger the audience, the more sympathetic to his poetry.

The ebbing tide of the Victorian age

"Did Poetry ever stand still?" Owen wrote to his cousin in 1918, when they had begun to diverge politically and poetically. "You can hark back if you like, and be deliberately archaic, but don't make yourself a lagoon, salved from the ebbing tide of the Victorian Age" (Letter 581). He was criticising not just Leslie's modest verses but what he himself had written as a teenager and might have gone on writing, if war and the Georgians had not intervened.

Leslie had just published a small book of poetry, *The Nymph*, dedicated to Wilfred in honour of their long literary collaboration. A verse of one poem, 'Hymn of Love to England', gives the flavour:

> O Mother! O England eternal!
> We sing to thee, sing to thy fame,
> Thy bounty, and beauty maternal,
> We sing to thy notable name.
> Though cruelly harried and hated
> By those that are loved not of thee,
> We praise thee with strength unabated
> Thyself and thy sea.

"I don't like 'Hymn of Love to England'", Wilfred commented, "naturally, at this period while I am composing 'Hymns of Hate'" (Letter 564). He was too kind to say that this was just the sort of "chiming sweetness" which he believed English poetry must learn to do without. By now he would have been embarrassed to re-read his own lines 'To Poesy' (his earliest surviving work), written at the age of about sixteen:

> A thousand suppliants stand around thy throne,
> Stricken with love for thee, O Poesy,
> I stand among them, and with them I groan,
> And stretch my arms for help. Oh, pity me!
> No man (save them thou gav'st the right to ascend
> And sit with thee, 'nointing with unction fine,
> Calling thyself their servant and their friend)
> Has loved thee with a purer love than mine.

And so on. Here is the archaic language, with its "thees" and "thous" and dropped syllables, which some people, even now, think suitable for poetry, and reading on we find "love" rhymed with "above", the references to "bards" and "maidens" which would annoy Yeats, and expressions like "meseems", "life's high meed", or "Cynthia" (for the moon). There are plenty of sixteen-year-olds today, we might think, who could write better. But the literary boy or girl today is exposed to a vast range of poetry, some of it in a modern idiom, and Wilfred did not have this advantage. He had not read the Metaphysicals, or Hardy, or the still obscure Hopkins. His idols were Keats and Shelley, whose influence can be seen in the lines just quoted; the subject-matter comes from *The Fall of Hyperion* and the groans and cries for help are reminiscent of Shelley's "I fall upon the thorns of life, I bleed" ('Ode to the West Wind'). The Romantics had been greatly admired all through the nineteenth century but their tradition was in decline, and would be killed off by the war. In Owen's childhood, the most popular poet was Tennyson, whose work is self-consciously "beautiful" and whose influence can be seen in 'Hospital Barge at Cerisy'. But he reacted against him after reading a biography which said that Tennyson was unhappy, "even in the midst of his fame, wealth, and domestic serenity" (Letter 538). Tennyson's emotional problems seemed trivial to anybody who had been on the Western Front.

'Lines Written on my Nineteenth Birthday' show a boy with real talent, but still struggling to express himself in an outdated mode. Like most teenagers, he is intensely self-absorbed. He wakes up on 18 March 1912, and a mysterious voice warns him:

> This night the final minute hath been laid
> Upon thy nineteen Springs. Aye, be dismayed
> To see the Fourth Part of thy utmost Span
> Now spent! What then? Affrighted dost thou plan
> To crowd the Rest with action, every whit?
> Ev'n so essay, but know thou canst not knit
> Thy web of hours so close as to regain
> E'en one lost stitch.

In the circumstances, this is a sad irony. The young man goes on to write a long rambling poem. He worries about the sufferings of the hungry and about his own failure to have achieved anything, misses his mother, reclines on his "couch of ruby velvet" (the vicar's sofa) and complains about "Torture's needles in the flesh" (indigestion). Only the last line and a half suggests that he can do something better:

> mounting higher still
> Into the dangerous air where actual Bliss doth thrill.

He did not mount but remained on a plateau for the next few years. At Dunsden and afterwards he was aware of real problems, like Violet, and his inability to find the work he wanted, but he could not write about them in clear comprehensible language. Instead he gave himself the task of versifying Hans Anderson's 'The Little Mermaid':

> Far out at sea, the water is as blue
> As cornflowers, and as clear as crystal-core;
> But so exceeding deep, no sea-bird's view
> Can fathom it, nor men's ropes touch its floor.
> Strange, snake-like trees and weeds — the same
>   which grew
> Before dry land with herbs was peopled o'er —
> Still sleep in heavy peacefulness down there,
> And hold their fluctuous arms towards upper air.
>
> And it is there the Sea-King's nation dwells.
> His palace, golden-bright and ruby-red,
> Gleams like a crown among those velvet dells.
> Pink, shimmering streams of light its windows shed,
> Like waterfalls of wine; and pink-white shells,
> Like Alpine snows, its lofty roof o'erspread;
> Which close and open, close and open wide,
> With every ebb and flowing of the tide.

He was nineteen; he would write in much the same way until he was twenty-four. He had no difficulty rhyming in the conventional manner and he had heeded Keats' advice to Shelley, "load every rift with ore". He has taken great pains to beautify his work; it contains nothing disturbing; he is very aware of colours and luxurious tastes or textures like wine or velvet. 'The Little Mermaid' has the occasional striking line — "like malt the surge was frothing", "the stunning guns are dumb". But on the whole, the smoothness and the attractive flow of images disguise the fact that he had nothing important to say.

Then came the war, which at first made little impact on his work. He wrote one poem, the 'Ballad of Peace and War':

> Fair days are yet left for the old
> And children's cheeks are ruddy,
> Because the good lads' limbs lie cold,
> And their brave cheeks are bloody

whose imagery he would reuse (in 'Inspection') with much greater power. 'Nocturne', written in France in 1915, shows that his social conscience was still active; as in 'Miners' the poet cannot relax because of the pain of others — "too many brains that rave in dust and steam". Meanwhile, as Europe fell apart, he, Leslie, and a young woman friend, Olwen Joergens, began exchanging sonnets on set subjects. As we can see from some titles — 'Purple', 'Music', 'Sunrise', 'Golden Hair' — these subjects were 'poetic' in the conventional sense and certainly did not address themselves to the war. The most remarkable poem in this series, begun in late 1916 before Wilfred went to the front line, was 'The End':

> After the blast of lightning from the east,
> The flourish of loud clouds, the Chariot Throne;
> After the drums of time have rolled and ceased,
> And by the bronze west long retreat is blown,
> Shall Life renew these bodies? Of a truth,
> All death will he annul, all tears assuage?
> Or fill these void veins full again with youth,
> And wash, with an immortal water, age?
>
> When I do ask white Age, he saith not so:
> 'My head hangs weighed with snow'.
> And when I hearken to the Earth, she saith:
> 'My fiery heart shrinks, aching. It is death.
> Mine ancient scars shall not be glorified,
> Nor my titanic tears, the sea, be dried'.

This is interesting if only because the fifth and sixth lines were eventually inscribed on his tombstone (with the second question mark removed). The poet is considering, not just the Christian Judgment Day, but also the Greek myth (in the story of Medea, for instance) that the old can be made young again by a magic potion. He clearly rejects both; death is real, pain and the aging process must not be 'glorified', the facts must be faced.

The closing lines are so sonorous and impressive that one is tempted not to think about their actual meaning (and Susan, apparently, chose to ignore it). They show how powerfully he could write by this time and also that, before he had seen it at close quarters, he was trying to accept the fact of death. He finished the sonnet after coming back from the front, and "these bodies" probably refer to those he had seen. But there is no direct engagement with the war.

'Happiness' was another title the three young poets had set themselves. He wrote the first version when behind the lines in February 1917, revised it at Craiglockhart, and told his mother that they were "the *only lines* of mine that carry the stamp of maturity" (Letter 538) so far:

> Ever again to breathe pure happiness,
> The happiness our mother gave us, boys?
> To smile at nothings, needing no caress?
> Have we not laughed too often since with joys?
> Have we not wrought too sick and sorrowful wrongs
> For her hands' pardoning? The sun may cleanse,
> And time, and starlight. Life will sing sweet songs,
> And gods will show us pleasures more than men's.
>
> Yet heaven looks smaller than the old doll's-home,
> No nestling place is left in bluebell bloom,
> And the wide arms of trees have lost their scope.
> The former happiness is unreturning:
> Boys' griefs are not so grievous as youth's yearning,
> Boys have no sadness sadder than our hope.

This was dedicated to his mother, and is a farewell to his boyhood. Jennifer Breen, in her edition of his *Selected Poetry and Prose* (1988, 2), suggests that one of Owen's strongest characteristics was "reverence for the maternal". This seems a real insight, for although the poet knows that the mother/child world is limited (how could Susan understand the horrors of the Western Front?), he is not happy to have moved beyond it. There is guilt here, as in later poems, and the flowers and trees will reappear in 'Spring Offensive' where nature, or mother earth, is vainly trying to rescue the self-doomed men. According to him, his maturity began when he had experienced war and realised just how much it clashed with the human and Christian values he had learned at his mother's knee.

Yet for some months longer he hesitated to write about what he had seen. And he kept the same style, writing another sonnet, 'With an Identity Disc' when in hospital with concussion:

> If ever I had dreamed of my dead name
> High in the heart of London, unsurpassed
> By Time for ever, and the Fugitive, Fame,
> There taking a long sanctuary at last, —
>
> Or if I onetime hoped to hide its shame,
> — Shame of success, and sorrow of defeats, —
> Under those holy cypresses, the same
> That shade always the quiet place of Keats,
>
> Now rather thank I God there is no risk
> Of gravers scoring it with florid screed.
> Let my inscription be this soldier's disc....
> Wear it, sweet friend, inscribe no date nor deed.
> But may thy heartbeat kiss it, night and day,
> Until the name grow blurred and fade away.

Having hoped to win undying fame like Keats (perhaps a memorial "high in the heart of London", in Westminster Abbey), he has renounced this ambition by joining the army where he is likely to be killed. He is too dissatisfied with himself and his poems to wish for any public memory. Instead, he urges the person who will receive his identity disc after death (in this case his brother Colin) to keep an affectionate private memory of him, which in time will die too. He was certainly thinking of Keats' epitaph for himself, "Here lies one whose name was writ in water". The irony is that Wilfred is remembered precisely because he accepted his fate and went to war.

But not because of poems like this. 'With an Identity Disc' is a fine and moving piece but, if he had died at this stage, he would not have been considered an important poet. He wrote one more sonnet, perhaps in his first weeks at Craiglockhart, which incidentally shows that, while shaken, he had not yet rejected the war:

ON SEEING A PIECE OF OUR HEAVY ARTILLERY
BROUGHT INTO ACTION

Be slowly lifted up, thou long black arm,
Great Gun towering towards Heaven, about to curse;
Sway steep against them, and for years rehearse
Huge imprecations like a blasting charm!
Reach at that Arrogance which needs thy harm,
And beat it down before its sins grow worse.
Spend our resentment, cannon, — yea, disburse
Our gold in shapes of flame, our breaths in storm.

Yet for men's sakes whom thy vast malison
Must wither innocent of enmity,
Be not withdrawn, dark arm, thy spoilure done,
Safe to the bosom of our prosperity.
But when thy spell be cast complete and whole,
May God curse thee, and cut thee from our soul!

This was one of his few descriptions, so far, of the battle zone, but blood, dirt, smells and suffering do not come into it. Instead he uses a host of abstract nouns — "arrogance", "resentment", "spoilure", "prosperity", and some very dated expressions like "disburse" and "malison", besides the archaic "thou" and "yea". All these sonnets show that he had developed great skill with words, but they are written in the 'poetic' language inherited from another century, and he cannot get closer to the war than by using the odd military image, a great gun, an identity disc. In the next few months he would stop writing sonnets — apart from his greatest, 'Anthem for Doomed Youth' — would loosen up his verse forms, and would let in a whole new range of sounds and images.

Not About Heroes: Siegfried Sassoon

Sassoon, whom Owen began to read perhaps not long after writing the 'artillery' sonnet, had started his career as a pleasant, minor Georgian. The poem previously mentioned, which had been considered worthy of going into *The Times*, had begun:

> Return to greet me, colours that were my joy,
> Not in the woeful crimson of men slain
> ('To Victory').

Graves had told him that he would soon change his style when he had been in the trenches. "Woeful crimson" was a woefully inadequate way of describing what bullets and shells could do to the human body. In a very short time he would radically reconstruct himself and his poetry, writing in his notebook in August 1916:

THE STUNT

> One night he crawled through wire and mud and found
>   a score
> Of Saxon peasants half-asleep, and wet and scared.
> Three men he killed outright, and wounded several more.
> But Gentle Jesus kept *him* safe; his life was spared.
> At dawn we took the trench; and found it full of dead.
> And for his deed the man received a D.S.O.
> 'How splendid. O how splendid!' his relations said,
> But what the weeping Saxons said I do not know.

This is certainly crude and unpolished; Sassoon himself did not think it worth printing. But it has the merit of shattering simplicity; any man in the trenches would immediately have responded to it as he would not have done to Owen's early work. The central ideas — that religion is being used to justify killing, that no one is guiltless, that soldiers on both sides have more in common with each other than with their relations — would become central in Owen's mind too. Sassoon said of his own work in a 1948 broadcast, "my trench-sketches were like rockets, sent up to illuminate the darkness. They were the first thing of their kind, and could

59

claim to be opportune". Reading them, Wilfred would have found descriptions of wire, sludge, rats, soldiers cursing and blaspheming, decent men getting killed and the seamier side of human nature. In 'The Hero', an officer tells soothing lies to the mother of a dead man who had really been a "cold-footed, useless swine". There is also a deep fury against civilians who make light of the troops' suffering; 'Blighters' is an attack on chorus girls who mock the dead by singing patriotic songs. Remembering his Dunsden experiences, Owen must have been especially struck by 'They', which has an affinity with his own poem 'The Chances':

> The Bishop tells us: 'When the boys come back
> 'They will not be the same; for they'll have fought
> 'In a just cause: they lead the last attack
> 'On Anti-Christ; their comrades' blood has bought
> 'New right to breed an honourable race,
> 'They have challenged Death and dared him face to face'.

> 'We're none of us the same!' the boys reply.
> 'For George lost both his legs; and Bill's stone blind;
> 'Poor Jim's shot through the lungs and like to die;
> 'And Bert's gone syphilitic: you'll not find
> 'A chap who's served that hasn't found *some* change'.
> And the Bishop said: 'The ways of God are strange!'

The artificial, high-flown language in verse 1, which echoes that of so many sermons and bad war poems, is starkly contrasted with the normal working men's speech and brutal frankness of verse 2. (Sassoon claimed this was the first time that a respectable poet had used the word "syphilitic"). It demonstrates his gift for the telling punch-line, a gift which Owen shared. Here, it is "the ways of God are strange", showing the Bishop's total inadequacy; in 'Lamentations', he would describe a man raving in agony because his brother had been killed and conclude, deadpan:

> Such men have lost all patriotic feeling.

Or there is the major in 'Base Details' who clucks over the casualty lists and then goes home to die — "in bed", or the 'One-Legged Man' who thinks, "Thank God they had to amputate!", or the famous last line of 'The General'. Hypocrisy is exposed, the contrast between those who talk and those who suffer brutally rammed home. Owen wrote after first reading them:

> Nothing like his trench life sketches has ever been written or ever will be written. Shakespeare reads vapid after these. Not of course because Sassoon is a greater artist, but because of the subjects, I mean. I think if I had the choice of making friends with Tennyson or with Sassoon I should go to Sassoon. (Letter 540)

It is often said that Sassoon was capable only of satire and anger while Owen wrote with a more profound and universal feeling, 'pity'. Sassoon himself, in the 1948 talk, generously recognised the younger man's greater talent, "It was Owen who revealed how, out of realistic horror and scorn, poetry might be born". But the distinction is too simple. Owen was also capable of anger and irony, and there is none in Sassoon's deeply-felt 'Sick Leave'. Of the poems in *The Old Huntsman*, Owen's favourite was 'The Death Bed', which describes a young man dying of wounds. It has the luxuriant, Keatsian quality of his own early poems — "amber light", "crimson gloom", "water — calm, sliding green" — and also his compassion for doomed youth. Like Owen in 'Futility', the poet stands beside the victim and longs to save him:

> He's young; he hated War; how should he die
> When cruel old campaigners win safe through?
>
> But death replied: 'I choose him'. So he went.

They had discovered that they shared the same bitter sorrow for war's victims. Through their work together in the next few months, their names would forever be joined.

....what the advanced composers are doing in music

Sassoon, though, had no influence on one feature of Owen's poetry; his development of half, or 'para' rhyme. When his work first appeared this was so unusual that there was almost more comment on the rhymes than the message; indeed the first critics saw a connection between them. Basil de Selincourt wrote:

> He invents a peculiar type of rhyme to aid him in the
> expression of that prevailing emotion of disgust, of weari-
> ness of illusion, of insistence on the bleak realities which he
> is determined to drive home. To put it briefly, he substitutes
> for vowel identity with its pleasing music, a consonantal
> identity which neither pleases nor is intended to please ...
> the intention is to chastise our sensibilities. (*Casebook*, 58-9)

John Middleton Murry thought Owen's half-rhymes "arose, not
from any desire to experiment for experiment's sake, but from the
inward need to say the thing he had to say most exactly and
finally". On the poem which he most admired, 'Strange Meeting',
he commented:

> The reader who comes fresh to this great poem does not
> immediately observe the assonant endings. At first he feels
> only that the blank verse has a mournful, impressive, even
> oppressive quality of its own; that the poem has a forged
> unity, a welded and inexorable massiveness. The emotion
> with which it is charged cannot be escaped; the meaning of
> the words and the beat of the sounds have the same
> indivisible message. The tone is single, low, muffled, sub-
> terranean. The reader looks again and discovers the techni-
> cal secret; but if he regards it then as an amazing technical
> innovation, he is in danger of falsifying his own reaction to
> the poem. Those assonant endings are indeed the discovery
> of genius; but in a truer sense the poet's emotion discovered
> them for itself. They are a dark and natural flowering of this,
> and only this, emotion. You cannot imagine them used for
> any other purpose save Owen's, or by any other hand save
> his. (*Casebook*, 61)

As a matter of fact, several of Owen's great poems — the majority,
perhaps — rhyme in the traditional way. But the half-rhymes
attracted comment because they were almost unheard-of in 1920,
and because one of the poems concerned was 'Strange Meeting'
(others are 'The Show', 'Insensibility', 'Exposure', 'Miners' and
'Futility'). Where he got the idea is still a matter for debate.

In his youth it had been taken for granted that poetry must be

written either in Miltonic blank verse, or with full rhymes.
"Moon" belonged naturally with "June"; "love" with "dove" or
"above" (although "move" was sometimes allowed). As the
typical bad poem now is a slab of prose cut up in lines, the typical
bad poem then was written in unnatural flowery language and
with rhymes that were entirely predictable. A good test of such
a poem is to read it aloud and see if the rhymes can be guessed
in advance (there is only a limited supply in English, so they
usually can). Sentences were wrenched out of shape, as in some
of Owen's early poems

> with them I groan

or

> when first that face I scanned

so that the desired word could be fitted in at the line's end. It all
added to the enormous distance from normal speech.

When half-rhyme is used, a whole new range of words becomes
available, as for instance "moon" may rhyme with — not "June"
— but "man", "mean", "mourn", "moan", or, more daringly,
"immune". These words all come from the last verse of 'Insensibility', where Owen discovered that the new technique gave him
far greater freedom. In this poem he tried stanzas of different
lengths, the occasional full rhyme and some lines that rhymed with
nothing, word-echoes in unexpected places ("whatever moans",
"whatever mourns"). Sometimes the vowel in the middle of a
word is changed instead of the consonant at the beginning:

> "killed/cold", "red/rid", "stuns/stones"

and sometimes there is a more unusual combination:

> "pack/ache", "march/dusk".

It also became easier to use longer words in the end-of-line
position. Whereas some double rhymes ("sorrow/morrow") had
been in use for many years, and become hackneyed, it was now
possible to try a simple change of vowel ("shelling/shilling"), or

a more subtle alteration ("brothers/withers"), or to use long and sonorous words which echoed one another:

"decimation/imagination/ammunition".

Poetry became more flexible and less predictable; the pattern of rhyme was changed, but not lost.

We know that Owen had been interested in half-rhyme well before he experienced war. Probably during his time in Bordeaux, in 1913 or 1914, he made a list of words for a projected poem — "land/learned/leaned/lined", "toll/toil/tool", and several more. The 'artillery' sonnet has a modest example; "arm", "charm" and "harm" rhyming, unexpectedly, with "storm". Soon after their first meeting he showed Sassoon an unimportant little poem, 'Song of Songs', which begins:

> Sing me at dawn but only with your laugh:
> Like sprightly Spring that laugheth into leaf;
> Like Love, that cannot flute for smiling at Life.

'Unimportant' because it says nothing of great interest, but it does show him developing a technique in which words echo each other within, as well as at the end of, a line:

"sprightly Spring", "laugheth/leaf"

and so on. Some readers, at least, were ready to accept this development; Sassoon liked the poem and persuaded him to put it in *The Hydra* and it was also published in a national magazine, *The Bookman*, the following year. The greatly superior 'Miners' was another of the few which appeared in Owen's lifetime. Leslie Gunston apparently told him it was not real poetry, to which he replied, "I suppose I am doing in poetry what the advanced composers are doing in music" (Letter 589).

Certainly some 'advanced' poets of his own age were already interested in moving away from traditional rhyme-patterns. Isaac Rosenberg had written:

> A worm fed on the heart of Corinth,
> Babylon and Rome.

Not Paris raped tall Helen,
But that incestuous worm.

Yet half-rhyme actually went back quite a long way, and Owen could have come across it in his reading. Henry Vaughan, on the other side of the border, had tried it out in the seventeenth century:

My soul, there is a country,
Far beyond the stars,
Where stands a winged sentry
All skilful in the wars.

He had not necessarily read Vaughan, and certainly not Hopkins whose own poetic experiments derived from the Welsh *cynghanedd*, "an ancient and intricate system of sound-chiming within a line of verse" (*Oxford Companion to the Literature of Wales*, 114). Hopkins had learned the Welsh language thoroughly, while Wilfred knew only a smattering of common words from two boyhood holidays. Nevertheless, there is evidence that he was interested in his Welsh roots.

This point is controversial because his sister Mary, writing in 1944, stated that although Owen is a Welsh name "we are an English family" (Welland, 107). But Harold believed that Welsh culture had had a profound effect on both parents and Wilfred, besides referring to "my forefathers the agile Welshmen of the Mountains" (Letter 663), ironically described Lloyd George, in a letter to his mother, as "our distinguished countryman" (Letter 480). In May 1918 he made notes for a project, "to write blank-verse plays on old Welsh themes". He was proud of his ancestry, Dominic Hibberd suggests, "because he held the Victorian view that imagination and strong, often melancholy emotions were Celtic endowments" (DH, 2). As Sven Backman has argued in an illuminating essay, Owen would not have needed to speak Welsh to find out about *cynghanedd*. He may also have discussed the question with Robert Graves, whose father was a crowned bard.

French poets were also trying out new rhyme schemes, and it has been suggested that Jules Romains could have influenced Owen, but there is no evidence that he had read him, although his library contains half a dozen books of French verse. Today he is popular in France, and his work has been translated into French verse.

Did he then invent half-rhyme himself, or stumble across it in French, Welsh or some other source? I believe the answer lies in an unpretentious book given to him at Dunsden at Christmas 1912 — *Elizabeth Barrett Browning and her Poetry* (1912), by Kathleen E. Royds. Her discussion of Mrs Browning's work states:

> Two of the poems quoted ... contain many instances of the peculiar rimes which Elizabeth Barrett frequently permitted herself to use; and which appear to justify a charge continually made against her, of slovenly workmanship, or at least of indifference.

She quotes examples like "deep in/leaping", "out/throat", "Bacchantes/grant us" from the poem 'Wine of Cyprus', and goes on:

> She was making experiments deliberately and of set purpose. Our earliest English poet, Chaucer, humorously lamented the paucity of rimes in the language; and many a poet, famed or unfamed, has doubtless suffered since from the same limitation. Elizabeth Barrett set herself to try to enlarge its possibilities. It is as a perfectly justifiable experiment that her attempt must be judged. But while she is freed from the charge of slovenly workmanship, it must be admitted that the device constitutes a flaw which obtrudes itself more and more on reperusal of the poems. That the trial, permissible in the first place, is not justified by its results, must be the final verdict (92-3).

This critic adds that Mrs Browning was a bad influence on young unpublished poets, who used half-rhymes in her style and then complained when their work was turned down.

Wilfred did not often mark his books, so there is no proof that he had seen this passage. But it is the one place where he is likely to have read a discussion of half-rhyme. Within two years of getting the book, as noted, he was jotting down lists of words like "land/learned/leaned/lined". He also owned a copy of Mrs Browning's *Complete Poems* which he was reading, and this time marking, at the casualty clearing station in March 1917. He copied a passage from *Aurora Leigh* which looks like blank verse but includes the line-endings "heat/hearts", "maids/birds", "verse/use", "take/lark" (Letter 497). In August he wrote to his mother from Craiglockhart:

> Yes, you will like to read Mrs Browning. Having
> listened so long to her low, sighing voice .... (Letter 538)

"So long" suggests that she was an old favourite. He goes on to say that her voice "*can* be *heard* often through the page". Anyone alert to sounds would have noticed her 'imperfect' rhymes; 'The Deserted Garden', for instance, contains the examples:

> "trees/sepulchres", "departed/deserted".

'De Profundis' plays on a series of rhymes for the word "on" including "stone", "tune", "done", "down", "unmown", and "impugn". He would certainly have known her celebrated 'Cry of the Children', would have sympathised with its appeal for exhausted child workers and might have noted the conjunction of "meadows/shadows", "forest/sorest", "tiring/iron", "onward/sunward", "unbelieving/disproving", and more. "Before you/glory" is the most audacious of these 'rhymes'. Two weeks after writing the above letter he reported that Sassoon liked his 'Song of Songs', and from then on he felt confident that a modern poet could, as he said to Nicholson, substitute "a play of vowels for pure rhyme" (Blunden 135).

It is also worth noting that Kathleen Royds spoke of Mrs Browning's "generous, large-souled championship of the downtrodden and the injured" (91). She had had passionate feelings on several issues, such as child labour, slavery and the liberation of Italy, and felt entitled to express them through her work. "She saw her poetry .... as a weapon", writes a modern biographer, " .... it was, to her, a form of direct action" (Margaret Forster, Introduction to *Selected Poems of Elizabeth Barrett Browning* [1988]). That had been controversial in her time too.

Possibly Clyde Black thought her suitable reading for Wilfred because her work is intensely Christian. *Casa Guidi Windows* suggests her vision of how men ought to live:

How to our races we may justify
Our individual claims, and, as we reach
Our own grapes, bend the top vines to supply
The children's uses, — how to fill a breach
With olive branches, — how to quench a lie
With truth, and smite a foe upon the cheek
With Christ's most conquering kiss.

To moderns, her work may seem old-fashioned and sentimental (although some of her sonnets will survive). But to Owen, beginning to think that poets should not be neutral, Mrs Browning, like Shelley and Sassoon, encouraged him to break with his old style of writing and speak his mind about the war. He would become the best known practitioner of her experiment with rhyme.

Owen and the Modernists

Today, of course, half-rhyme does not shock. Indeed, most published poetry now uses no rhyme whatever, so a critic can write that "free verse spread like a latter-day Black Death throughout the poetries of Europe .... destroying with a casual negligence the great work of time", in the aftermath of the Great War. He says of the pioneers — Eliot, Pound and William Carlos Williams:

> In essence they took away from poetry what had always been its distinguishing and defining characteristic, metre, and offered in metre's place nothing which prose could not already accomplish much better. The result has been an art form in an extreme state of collapse and prey to every passing mountebank's whim. It seems safe to say that poetry has *never*, not in the history of mankind's literacy, been so little read or attended to, it has never meant less to the general literate public. If it dies it will be the fault of those who tried in the first years of this century to revive it by leaching it of its identity. (Dick Davis, 'The Revolt against Metre', *Poetry Durham* Number 28)

However necessary the modernist revolt was, it remains true that the common reader values metre and above all rhyme, feeling that poetry is somehow not poetry without it. From nursery rhymes to advertising jingles and the wretched verses in birthday cards, there is a sense of satisfaction when words echo one another convincingly. It is interesting that Owen did not often write blank verse, and when he did it was not among his best work.

It is also true that the general reader has problems understanding modern poetry. At the bottom end of the scale, we have 'poems' which are merely commonplace prose arranged in lines; at the top, T.S. Eliot saying that because we live in a complex society poetry 'must be difficult'. Small wonder if many amateurs still try to write in a style that was popular before the Great War.

Where does Owen fit in? Having been avant-garde in his own day, he now seems quite traditional; Desmond Graham in *The Truth of War* (1984) reports that some academics look down on him for being 'easy'. His typical work is stately and mellifluous; he loved rhyme and was not willing to give it up; he very much wished to be understood by the common reader. "Is this worth going on with?" he wrote to Sassoon about 'Spring Offensive' six weeks before he was killed. "I don't want to write anything to which a soldier would say No Compris!" On the other hand Yeats, 'the last Romantic', denounced him, while Eliot and other innovating poets always spoke of him with respect.

His contacts with the Modernists came very late, in the summer of 1918. Osbert Sitwell had already met him and they got on because of their anti-war views. Having read 'Mental Cases', he and Edith requested more poems for *Wheels*, and Wilfred went to some trouble to find a copy. The 1917 anthology is very rare, but can be seen today with his other books in the English Library at Oxford. Comprising nine young poets, six men and three women, it proudly quoted reviews which emphasised its newness and strangeness. "Precious", "macabre", "Baudelairean" are some of the epithets hurled at them, and it was alternatively called the "vanguard of British poetry" or blamed for "morbid eccentricity". The poems ranged from ultra-modern work by Aldous Huxley:

> My typewriter has been writing crookedly
> For a very considerable time
> ('Farewell to the Muses')

to Osbert Sitwell's 'Armchair', a Sassoon-like poem which parodied the 'grand old men' in charge of the war:

If I were old, or only seventy,
Then should I be a great man in his prime.
I should rule army-corps: at my command
Men would rise up, salute me, and attack
— And die — Or I might also govern men
By making speeches with my toothless jaws ....
That day I'd send my grandsons out to France
— And wish I'd got ten other ones to send
(One cannot sacrifice too much, I'd say!)
Then would I make a noble, toothless speech
And all the list'ning parliament would cheer.
'Gentlemen, we will never end this war
Till all the younger men with martial mien
Have entered capitals; never make peace
Till they are cripples, on one leg, or dead!'
Then would the Bishops all go mad with joy ....
In every pulpit they would preach and prance; ....
Then we'd forbid all Liberty and make
Free speech a relic of our impious past;
And when this war is finished, when the world
Is torn and bleeding, cut and bruised to death,
Then I'd pronounce my peace terms — to the poor!

Osbert had also written an epigram on Clemenceau, and Wilfred, perhaps, recalled both poems when he parodied the old man's "noble, toothless speech" in 'Smile, Smile, Smile'. The Sitwells and their friends were ironic, melancholy, obsessed with urban scenes. Their work had some influence on his late, unfinished poem, 'The Roads Also'.

Today he is often compared (not always favourably) with Isaac Rosenberg, who was killed in the same year without either of them having had the chance to read the other. Rosenberg's great poem, 'Break of Day in the Trenches', published in the United States at the end of 1916, is written with a quite different sensibility from Sassoon's and Owen's:

Droll rat, they would shoot you if they knew
Your cosmopolitan sympathies ....
Now you have touched this English hand
You will do the same to a German —

70

It is an entirely modern poem, rhymeless — though with its own metre beating away behind the lines — laid-back, requiring more than one reading before it yields up its full meaning. The poet is well aware that war is murderous but shows no particular outrage, nor does he seem much concerned about his own situation. He just notes quietly (through the pretence of having a rat tried for treason) that it is absurd.

Owen is now read more widely than any other war poet (and Rosenberg's stature, too, is growing). People who have never been near a battlefield, including children, respond to him because they know he is writing about something vital and because, for all his experimenting, he never lost touch with the common reader. Philip Hobsbaum argued, in 1961, that English poetry had been deformed by the historical accident of Owen, Rosenberg and Edward Thomas, who were all "developing an essentially English modernity", having been killed before they made their mark. The three poets, all aged under forty, were extremely different, but had each in his own way recognised "the need to adapt the old forms to express new experience". Afterwards Pound and Eliot started

> an essentially American revolution in verse technique over here rather than in the United States, and so filled the gap which the death of the war poets left with an alien product whose influence has been a bad one.... If Thomas, Owen and Rosenberg had lived, there would have been no question of having to choose between revolution and reaction.... What is best in English poetry generally is what we find in the uncompleted work of these three poets: what Thom Gunn called 'vigour within the discipline of shape'. Freedom won, that is, not through breaking down a form but through reshaping it. These poets represent the central line of English poetry through the Romantics back to Shakespeare. ('The Road Not Taken', *Casebook* 101-8).

I have a lot of sympathy with this viewpoint, but it is now impossible to guess what course English poetry would have taken if there had been no war, or if the best young poets had not been killed. That belongs, as 'Strange Meeting' says, to "the undone years".

The poems which follow were all written in Owen's *annus*

mirabilis between August 1917 and the autumn of 1918. Some of them overlap, because he went back and revised them constantly. I have departed from strict chronological order on occasion, but the time-sequence is roughly right.

The first draft of 'The Dead-Beat' was written at Craiglockhart, soon after Owen had read and met Sassoon, and it marks an enormous change of style:

THE DEAD-BEAT

He dropped, — more sullenly than wearily,
Lay stupid like a cod, heavy like meat,
And none of us could kick him to his feet;
— Just blinked at my revolver, blearily;
— Didn't appear to know a war was on,
Or see the blasted trench at which he stared.
'I'll do 'em in', he whined. 'If this hand's spared,
I'll murder them, I will'.   .
                    A low voice said,
'It's Blighty, p'raps, he sees; his pluck's all gone,
Dreaming of all the valiant, that *aren't* dead:
Bold uncles, smiling ministerially;
Maybe his brave young wife, getting her fun
In some new home, improved materially.
It's not these stiffs have crazed him; nor the Hun'.

We sent him down at last, out of the way.
Unwounded; — stout lad, too, before that strafe.
Malingering? Stretcher-bearers winked, 'Not half!'

Next day I heard the Doc's well-whiskied laugh:
'That scum you sent last night soon died. Hooray!'

This is deliberately 'unpoetic', low-key, using trench slang ("stiffs" for corpses, "Blighty" for England — the word was also used to mean a slight wound which would ensure a passage home). It was the first of a series of poems which would describe the underside of war. Apparently it was based on a real happening and the first version used the doctor's actual words.

The man is made to sound thoroughly unappealing; the words "cod" and "meat" suggesting flesh without spirit. Owen when he first reached the front had described the common soldiers as "expressionless lumps" (Letter 476), an opinion which he would revise. His companions kick him; Owen himself appears as the officer who threatens to shoot him unless he pulls himself together. Only the disembodied "low voice" makes us aware of what is wrong, and hints that the "them" he is impotently threatening may not be the Germans, as we suppose.

Again and again, in contemporary accounts, we find those who had been in France showing extreme hostility to those on the home front who appeared indifferent to their suffering. These people are identified as the real enemy; "the valiant, that *aren't* dead" are loud-mouthed non-combatants; "bold uncles, smiling ministerially" are men above military age who give statesmanlike speeches about fighting to the bitter end. The reference to the man's wife is one of several which seem hostile to women, but that will be considered in the next chapter.

In the last line comes a shocking illumination. The man is not wounded, and had apparently been normal before the bombing, but suddenly we hear that he has died. The reason is not at all clear but we assume that his entire system has collapsed under pressure, "foreheads of men have bled where no wounds were". As someone who had also collapsed without being physically hurt, Owen was well placed to understand his condition. The Doc, like the clerics in later poems, has betrayed his profession, but the poet enlarges our sympathies, forcing us to see that this unlikeable man is a human being with rights, which have been violated, and that no one may condemn him if they have not been through the same ordeal.

'The Chances' is another poem in the tough, colloquial style of Sassoon:

THE CHANCES

> I mind as how the night before that show
> Us five got talkin'; we was in the know.
> 'Ah well', says Jimmy, and he's seen some scrappin',
> 'There ain't no more than five things as can happen,—
> You get knocked out; else wounded, bad or cushy;
> Scuppered; or nowt except you're feelin' mushy'.

One of us got the knock-out, blown to chops;
One lad was hurt, like, losin' both his props;
And one — to use the word of hypocrites —
Had the misfortune to be took by Fritz.
Now me, I wasn't scratched, praise God Almighty,
Though next time please I'll thank him for a blighty.
But poor old Jim, he's livin' and he's not;
He reckoned he'd five chances, and he had:
He's wounded, killed, and pris'ner, all the lot,
The flamin' lot all rolled in one. Jim's mad.

This has obviously been inspired by Sassoon's 'They'. The form is very similar; both poems are based on working-class speech and each has a group of men describing the different appalling things which have happened to them. Both are starkly realist and accessible. But a close comparison shows that Owen had already gone beyond his master. 'They' is highly effective satire but the bishop, perhaps, is too easy a target, and the last line ("And the Bishop said, 'The ways of God are strange!'" while satisfying, tells us nothing we did not already know. In 'The Chances' the tension mounts steadily — we want to know what happened — and the last word of the last line delivers a shattering blow.

Making the working classes speak, dropped aitches and all, is a task which most educated writers manage badly. Owen's successive drafts show that he steadily improved the poem, getting rid of comic misspellings and bringing it as close as possible to ordinary written English, although it remains the speech of an unpretentious man. There is slang, but only one word, "scuppered" (captured), is likely to give trouble to modern readers. It is devastatingly simple and effective.

The poem begins with five men, five chances. The likelihood of survival was endlessly discussed in the trenches, with views ranging from predestination — "a bullet gets you if it has your name on"— to the belief that you would not be killed if you did the right things, perhaps obeying God. In fact it was probably a matter of "chance's strange arithmetic" ('Insensibility'), or what we would call being in the wrong place at the wrong time. Three of the five friends come to grief.

The first man is "blown to chops", a deliberately brutal phrase suggesting he is now no more than butcher's meat. The second is "hurt, like"; the narrator using understatement until we reach the end of the line and the word "props", which even we know means "legs". The third is taken prisoner and those who call this a "misfortune" are "hypocrites"; the man is obviously well out of it. The fourth survives to tell the tale (but would prefer a wound to taking his chances again). Finally Jim, who thought that there were only five options, suffers a fate he had never dreamed of; it had not been discussed because the conventional attitude to war assumes that heroes don't go mad. The word, which hits us at the very end of the poem, is so shocking that we now only use it as a joke, preferring to find gentler descriptions for a mangled psyche. We are to think of Jim as mad permanently, in prison for life. In later poems, 'S.I.W' and 'Mental Cases', Owen would continue to explore what the war experience could do to a man's mind. He would also go on, from this very successful poem in Sassoon's manner, to find a language of his own, as in his final, magnificent sonnet:

ANTHEM FOR DOOMED YOUTH

What passing-bells for these who die as cattle?
— Only the monstrous anger of the guns.
Only the stuttering rifles' rapid rattle
Can patter out their hasty orisons.
No mockeries now for them; no prayers nor bells;
Nor any voice of mourning save the choirs, —
The shrill, demented choirs of wailing shells;
And bugles calling for them from sad shires.

What candles may be held to speed them all?
Not in the hands of boys but in their eyes
Shall shine the holy glimmers of goodbyes.
The pallor of girls' brows shall be their pall;
Their flowers the tenderness of patient minds,
And each slow dusk a drawing-down of blinds.

Sassoon, who worked with Owen on the many revisions of this poem, wrote afterwards of its "classic and imaginative serenity". "I now realised that his verse, with its sumptuous epithets and large-scale imagery, its noble naturalness and depth of meaning,

had impressive affinities with Keats, whom he took as his supreme exemplar" (SJ 59-60). Keats is certainly present in line 7,
which recalls "Then in a wailful choir the small gnats mourn"
from 'To Autumn'. But Sassoon also helped, suggesting "patient"
to replace "silent" in the penultimate line. It shows how far
Owen's work and thought had developed, once he was in regular
contact with another poet. His own sonorous language, mastery
of form and tendency to "load every rift with ore" unite with his
new ability to write about what he had seen at the front.

The language is not transparent, as in the last two poems, which
are mainly concerned with telling a significant story. It is incanta-
tory, ritualistic, an elegy for his generation. Owen had hinted in
letters home that what upset him most was "the dead, whose
unburiable bodies sit outside the dug-outs all day, all night, the
most execrable sights on earth. In poetry we call them the most
glorious. But to sit with them all day, all night ... and a week later
to come back and find them still sitting there, in motionless groups,
THAT is what saps the 'soldierly spirit'" (Letter 482). He was now
struggling to write poetry which could come to terms with that
experience.

It is not a 'protest poem'; the word "monstrous" may suggest
the poet's own anger but he does not suggest that any particular
person is responsible for the killing or that it could be stopped.
Nevertheless, if we compare it with Brooke's sonnet 'The Dead'
(which Owen knew) we notice that he does not talk about nobility
or sacrifice. Nor does he, like Laurence Binyon in 'For the Fallen'
(also known to him) say such things as

> They were staunch to the end against odds uncounted
> They fell with their faces to the foe.

The dead are just victims, "these who die as cattle"; the killing
fields have no more glory than a giant abattoir. This makes
'Anthem' significantly different from other elegies for dead youth.
His theme is the near-impossibility of coping with death on such
a scale. In peacetime, even one death causes an enormous upheaval and is accompanied by all kinds of rituals — the passing-bell,
rung once for each year of life in country districts, prayers, candles,
flowers, mourning clothes, black-edged notepaper and the draw-

ing-down of blinds in the bereaved house. Some of these practices are now obsolete but most of us still need a ceremony of some sort to come to terms with death. But here, Owen says, the world has become "demented"; not only are men being killed like cattle but many of the dead are denied burial and the survivors have no time to mourn properly. The first eight lines set out the situation; the last six consider what response is possible.

His answer is that prayers and bells are "mockeries", often insincere and in any case not adequate given the vastness of the tragedy. Later poems, like 'Disabled' and 'The Send-Off', would suggest a distrust of public ritual, and by this time he had ceased to believe in the resurrection of the dead. They could live on only in the remembrance of those who truly loved them, "the tenderness of patient minds". We get an impression of younger brothers holding back tears, of girls grown pale from sorrow and anxiety. Dominic Hibberd suggests that they "may be *femmes fatales*, luring youth to its doom" (DH 112). If the poem is saying that, it is unfair; whoever was responsible for the war, it was not girls. But I do not detect any irony in these lines. Owen is saying that grief goes on for years, that it is "silent" or "patient", and that it cannot be affected by what happens to the body after death. He closes with the majestic line

And each slow dusk a drawing-down of blinds.

This is long-drawn-out by the power of half-rhyme and alliteration, "each/dusk","slow/draw","dusk/drawing-down/blinds". The sounds echo one another, and then die away. Owen does not say, like Binyon:

At the going down of the sun and in the morning
We will remember them

but he does evoke the idea of evening, traditionally a time of melancholy, giving way to night, which means death. Darkness shrouds the western front and the whole of nature is in mourning for her children. These are the only kinds of mourning that are possible.

In his next poem, pity and anger are knitted together inextric-

right ably. The Latin title (from Horace) means, "It is sweet and becoming to die for the fatherland", and it would have been familiar to any educated person in those days. Along with "Greater love hath no man than this" (treated in another poem), "dulce et decorum est" became one of the best-known quotations of the war. Owen dedicated the first version to Jessie Pope, of *Punch*, whose other claim to fame is that she edited the first, mangled version of Robert Tressell's *Ragged-Trousered Philanthropists*. She had not apparently said that dying was "dulce et decorum", but she did write some silly verses urging young men to enlist. Here is Owen's poem:

DULCE ET DECORUM EST

Bent double, like old beggars under sacks,
Knock-kneed, coughing like hags, we cursed through
    sludge,
Till on the haunting flares we turned our backs
And towards our distant rest began to trudge.
Men marched asleep. Many had lost their boots
But limped on, blood-shod. All went lame; all blind;
Drunk with fatigue; deaf even to the hoots
Of tired, outstripped Five-Nines that dropped behind.

Gas! GAS! Quick, boys! — An ecstasy of fumbling,
Fitting the clumsy helmets just in time;
But someone still was yelling out and stumbling,
And flound'ring like a man in fire or lime ....
Dim, through the misty panes and thick green light,
As under a green sea, I saw him drowning.

In all my dreams, before my helpless sight,
He plunges at me, guttering, choking, drowning.

If in some smothering dreams you too could pace
Behind the wagon that we flung him in,
And watch the white eyes writhing in his face,
His hanging face, like a devil's sick of sin;
If you could hear, at every jolt, the blood
Come gargling from the froth-corrupted lungs,
Obscene as cancer, bitter as the cud
Of vile, incurable sores on innocent tongues,—

My friend, you would not tell with such high zest
To children ardent for some desperate glory,
The old Lie: Dulce et decorum est
Pro patria mori.

The poet takes his time before coming to the central point. In the first verse, he describes a hellish landscape, lit only by what he calls "haunting flares", in a haunting phrase. The Five-Nines are 5.9 shells. The army is in retreat, wanting only to rest; some men marching in their sleep (this really happened), and all lame, blind, and deaf. The suggestion is that they are sleepwalking to their doom and that the blind are leading the blind, which according to the Bible means that "all shall fall into the ditch". But the real horror is yet to come.

While they are off guard, there is a gas attack and the poem gives way to reported speech, "Gas! GAS! Quick, boys!" and the amazing words "ecstasy of fumbling" which describe a frantic race against time. But one man is too slow, and is poisoned by the fumes. The poet sees this happening and knows he will be haunted all his life by his inability to save him. The word "drowning" (not "drowned") is placed emphatically at the end of the line, and comes twice, to stress that it keeps on happening in the witness's mind. The metaphors are surprisingly beautiful, thick green light and a green sea, although there is no natural green anywhere at the front. Their classic calm contrasts with the ugliness of death by gassing.

For, apparently, the man takes some time to die, and we are forced to watch him. His lungs are "corrupted" and the corruption extends far beyond him, including to our language. Owen deliberately uses the most shocking words he can think of, and his editors did not print "obscene as cancer" for over forty years. Cancer, the C-word, which many people even now do not like to say and which was usually referred to then as "a malignant disease". The sores on youthful tongues (he seems to have been thinking of venereal disease) are another peculiarly intimate and shaming type of pain. It is necessary to write these things down, because nothing else will jolt his readers out of their complacency.

Yet Owen remains in full control of his material, unlike, say, some Vietnam poets who scattered casual obscenities everywhere and who did not use traditional forms. The Latin is fully integrated into the poem, rhyming effortlessly ("zest/est", "story/mori") with the two lines that come before. One of his objects was to make it impossible for this phrase ever to be taken seriously again, and, indeed, it never has been. He was surely right, too, to drop the reference to Jessie Pope which would have dated within a few years. "My friend" stands for anyone, in his time or ours, who glorifies or speaks lightly of death in war. To them the poem says, *"if you could hear, if you could see"*.

"Disabled" is another Craiglockhart poem which may have been suggested by something Owen had seen in Edinburgh; the central figure has been in a Scottish regiment and the park could be Princes Street gardens. Whether or not, we are to imagine a dreadfully disabled young man — at least three limbs are missing — "parked" in his wheelchair while the rest of the world is out enjoying itself:

DISABLED

He sat in a wheeled chair, waiting for dark,
And shivered in his ghastly suit of grey,
Legless, sewn short at elbow. Through the park
Voices of boys rang saddening like a hymn,
Voices of play and pleasure after day,
Till gathering sleep had mothered them from him.

About this time Town used to swing so gay
When glow-lamps budded in the light blue trees,
And girls glanced lovelier as the air grew dim, —
In the old times, before he threw away his knees.
Now he will never feel again how slim
Girls' waists are, or how warm their subtle hands.
All of them touch him like some queer disease.

There was an artist silly for his face,
For it was younger than his youth, last year.
Now, he is old; his back will never brace;
He's lost his colour very far from here,
Poured it down shell-holes till the veins ran dry,
And half his lifetime lapsed in the hot race
And leap of purple spurted from his thigh.

One time he liked a blood-smear down his leg,
After the matches, carried shoulder-high.
It was after football, when he'd drunk a peg,
He thought he'd better join. — He wonders why.
Someone had said he'd look a god in kilts,
That's why; and maybe, too, to please his Meg,
Aye, that was it, to please the giddy jilts
He asked to join. He didn't have to beg;
Smiling they wrote his lie: aged nineteen years.
Germans he scarcely thought of; all their guilt
And Austria's, did not move him. And no fears
Of Fear came yet. He thought of jewelled hilts
For daggers in plaid socks; of smart salutes;
And care of arms; and leave; and pay arrears;
Esprit de corps; and hints for young recruits.
And soon, he was drafted out with drums and cheers.

Some cheered him home, but not as crowds cheer Goal.
Only a solemn man who brought him fruits
Thanked him; and then enquired about his soul.

Now, he will spend a few sick years in institutes,
And do what things the rules consider wise,
And take whatever pity they may dole.
Tonight he noticed how the women's eyes
Passed from him to the strong men that were whole.
How cold and late it is! Why don't they come
And put him into bed? Why don't they come?

Part of the greatness of this poem is that Owen has succeeded in creating a man who, before the disaster, was far closer to the norm than himself. He is some years younger than the poet and much less intelligent, did not think about the reasons for the war and was mainly interested in women and football. There is a distinct resemblance to Housman's 'To an Athlete Dying Young':

That time you won your town the race
We chaired you through the market-place;
Man and boy stood cheering by,
And home we brought you shoulder-high.

Today, the road all runners come,

Shoulder-high we bring you home,
And set you at your threshold down,
Townsman of a stiller town.

But the great difference between Housman's athlete and this one is that the man did not die. Death fits easily into the heroic stereotype but when a man survives, hideously mutilated, he becomes an embarrassment. It is normal to turn our eyes away from him, to say that he would be better dead; the wounded were excluded from the Falklands thanksgiving service because they undermined myths about war. Of course, this attitude is very widespread and extends to anyone who is physically or mentally less than perfect. It is perhaps worth noting that, in Shrewsbury, the Owen family had known a young man with a serious speech impediment and had made a special effort to be friendly to him. Wilfred had taken little notice in those days but, as the poem shows, his parents' values had stuck.

The man has "lost his colour" and wears a ghastly, institutional grey suit. Light blue trees? They sound improbable, but show him to be surrounded by a landscape of bright colours, light and movement where he is grotesquely out of place. This reminds him of the time when he took all these things for granted, and his story, a typical one, emerges in the fourth section. It was natural for a warm-blooded young man to join the army after a few drinks, thinking it was no more serious than a game of football, but this does not excuse those who allowed and encouraged his mistake. They include the recruiting sergeant — "He didn't have to beg", the poem says dryly — his girl friend, and the cheering crowds. When he comes back limbless the cheers are fainter; "Meg" is no longer around and even those who are supposed to be caring for him have gone elsewhere. Having thrown away all he valued, what he gets instead is a man inquiring about his soul. Sassoon describes how, when he was brought home wounded, he was given "a leaflet by the Bishop of London who earnestly advised me to lead a clean life and attend Holy Communion" (*Memoirs of an Infantry Officer*, 8, 5). Both poets found this attitude impudent and patronising.

But the reference to the man's soul is not quite pointless. Having lived entirely through the body, he is not able to adapt to disability as, perhaps, Owen himself might have done, and the last verse suggests that he will not be an embarrassment for much longer. He is waiting not just for the dark, but for death. The total effect is to make us revalue a life which might have seemed uninteresting before the tragedy, useless afterwards. Owen takes us inside his legless suit and compels us to see the world as it was for him; "the poetry is in the pity".

The last four poems are all written in conventional rhyme but, by the time Owen finished 'Insensibility', he had thoroughly mastered the technique of half-rhyme — "feet/fought", "stars/shores" — and was using it with great skill. The free-flowing stanzas, of varying lengths, are another break with traditional poetry; the strong end-rhymes come not where the reader expects them but where they will have the greatest effect. Indeed he suggests, in the first verse, that a lot of poetry is no more than "tearful fooling", which means that if his own poetry is going to be worth anything it will have to break some rules.

INSENSIBILITY

1
Happy are men who yet before they are killed
Can let their veins run cold.
Whom no compassion fleers
Or makes their feet
Sore on the alleys cobbled with their brothers.
The front line withers.
But they are troops who fade, not flowers,
For poets' tearful fooling:
Men, gaps for filling:
Losses, who might have fought
Longer, but no one bothers.

2
And some cease feeling
Even themselves or for themselves.
Dullness best solves
The tease and doubt of shelling,
And Chance's strange arithmetic
Comes simpler than the reckoning of their shilling.
They keep no check on armies' decimation.

3
Happy are these who lose imagination:
They have enough to carry with ammunition.
Their spirit drags no pack.
Their old wounds, save with cold, can not more ache.
Having seen all things red,
Their eyes are rid
Of the hurt of the colour of blood for ever.
And terror's first constriction over,
Their hearts remain small-drawn.
Their senses in some scorching cautery of battle
Now long since ironed,
Can laugh among the dying, unconcerned.

4
Happy the soldier home, with not a notion
How somewhere, every dawn, some men attack,
And many sighs are drained.
Happy the lad whose mind was never trained:
His days are worth forgetting more than not.
He sings along the march
Which we march taciturn, because of dusk,
The long, forlorn, relentless trend
From larger day to huger night.

5
We wise, who with a thought besmirch
Blood over all our soul,
How should we see our task
But through his blunt and lashless eyes?
Alive, he is not vital overmuch;
Dying, not mortal overmuch;
Nor sad, nor proud,
Nor curious at all.
He cannot tell
Old men's placidity from his.

6
But cursed are dullards whom no cannon stuns,
That they should be as stones.
Wretched are they, and mean
With paucity that never was simplicity.
By choice they made themselves immune

To pity and whatever moans in man
Before the last sea and·the hapless stars;
Whatever mourns when many leave these shores;
Whatever shares
The eternal reciprocity of tears.

The theme continues that of 'Anthem for Doomed Youth'; how can any reaction match up to the scale of the slaughter? As George Eliot said, "if we had a keen vision and feeling of all ordinary human life it would be like hearing the grass grow and the squirrel's heart beat, and we should die of that roar which lies on the other side of silence. As it is, the quickest of us walk about well wadded with stupidity" (*Middlemarch*, Chapter 20). Owen is contrasting his own nervous breakdown with the fact that other men have grown accustomed to war. They have old wounds (not necessarily physical) but can live with them, and they seem to be unmoved by their friends' deaths and their own extreme danger. War itself is not described; we just get an impression of long, pointless, dreary marching and indescribable horrors — "having seen all things red ... the hurt of the colour of blood".

The poet says that "we wise" — those who write and read poems — have a greater capacity for suffering than the man "whose mind was never trained". This seems to me a very doubtful argument. It is true that several intellectuals are chronic worriers, but education cannot affect the capacity to feel or not feel pain. To be more accurate, there is a large section of the population which suffers intensely, in or out of war, while others cope reasonably well with the same stresses. Owen knew himself to belong to the sensitive minority; it took only a "thought" for his consciousness to be smirched with blood. In 'Mental Cases' he would write about men who were in an even worse state than himself, "Sunlight seems a blood-smear; night comes blood-black".

If the ordinary man had been stunned into insensibility, one could only be glad for his sake; it is rather like giving drink or tranquillisers to a man about to be hanged. (The war might have stopped, if they had all fully realised what was happening, but the poem does not explore that possibility). However, the last verse expresses a terrible anger, saying that those who are not exposed to the horrors and do not care about them cannot be forgiven.

"Paucity", which means littleness of heart and mind, is not the same as the rhyming word "simplicity". Generals and bloodthirsty civilians, who perhaps say that the men in the trenches are happy, have chosen to have no normal feeling for others. They all seem to be located in England, from which thousands are being shipped out, never to return. His own passionate belief is that "reciprocity" — instinctive sympathy, often expressed through tears — is an essential human duty.

The poem is, then, saying the opposite of what it appears to be saying in the first five verses. Men under pressure may lose imagination; those who mould public opinion, including poets, must not.

"He was one of those to whom the miseries of the world are misery and will not let them rest", wrote Frank Nicholson (Blunden 135). The quote is from Keats' 'Fall of Hyperion', which Owen practically knew by heart. It is a dialogue between the poet, who wishes to heal "the giant agony of the world", but feels helpless, and the prophetess, Moneta, who expresses scorn for the little-minded:

> All else who find a haven in the world,
> Where they may thoughtless sleep away their days,
> If by a chance into this fane they come,
> Rot on the pavement where thou rottedst half.

Owen's judgment on such people was that they were "wretched", "mean", and "cursed". On the whole, history agrees with him about those responsible for the Great War.

'The Show' begins with an epitaph from a living poet he admired, W.B. Yeats:

> We have fallen in the dreams the ever-living
> Breathe on the tarnished mirror of the world,
> And then smooth out with ivory hands and sigh.

and goes on to give one of his grimmest pictures of the front:

THE SHOW

My soul looked down from a vague height, with Death,

As unremembering how I rose or why,
And saw a sad land, weak with sweats of dearth,
Grey, cratered like the moon with hollow woe,
And pitted with great pocks and scabs of plagues.

Across its beard, that horror of harsh wire,
There moved thin caterpillars, slowly uncoiled.
It seemed they pushed themselves to be as plugs
Of ditches, where they writhed and shrivelled, killed.

By them had slimy paths been trailed and scraped
Round myriad warts that might be little hills.

From gloom's last dregs these long-strung creatures crept,
And vanished out of dawn down hidden holes.

(And smell came up from those foul openings
As out of mouths, or deep wounds deepening.)

On dithering feet upgathered, more and more,
Brown strings, towards strings of grey, with bristling
    spines,
All migrants from green fields, intent on mire.

Those that were gray, of more abundant spawns,
Ramped on the rest and ate them and were eaten.

I saw their bitten backs curve, loop, and straighten.
I watched those agonies curl, lift and flatten.

Whereat, in terror what that sight might mean,
I reeled and shivered earthward like a feather.

And Death fell with me, like a deepening moan,
And He, picking a manner of worm, which half had hid
Its bruises on the earth, but crawled no further,
Showed me its feet, the feet of many men,
And the fresh-severed head of it, my head.

"Show" is slang for a great battle. The Yeats quotation deals with
the gods who observe men fighting but take little interest in their
fate.

This is an extraordinary poem. Less perfect than some (for the half-rhyme in "why/woe/wire", sounds shaky) it is outstanding for its vision of a world in torment, and for the fear it evokes. There are two sources. Sassoon was enthusiastic about Hardy's *The Dynasts*, a verse-play about the last great European upheaval, in Napoleon's time, and had urged his friend to read it. Owen would certainly have shared Hardy's viewpoint, expressed by the Spirit of the Pities:

> Each for himself, his family, his heirs;
> For the wan weltering nations who concerns, who cares?
> (Part First, Act 6, Scene 5)

Hardy's spirits look down "from a vague altitude" (see Owen's "vague height"). They see "the peoples, distressed by events which they did not cause ... writhing, crawling, heaving and vibrating in their various cities and nationalities". Napoleon's army in retreat from Russia was conceived as a caterpillar, getting thinner as men dropped away. The other influence was Henri Barbusse (1873-1935), author of *Le Feu*. Barbusse, a militant Socialist, had based this novel on his trench experiences, and it says much for freedom of speech in wartime France that it was not only published but awarded the Goncourt Prize. It was published in English in 1917 as *Under Fire, the Story of a Squad*. Sassoon introduced it to Owen (there is a French copy in his library), who said that it "set him alight as no other war book had done" (SJ 60).

Barbusse wrote frankly about the horrors of war and the need for solidarity between people from all countries. He, too, had described the armies as "crawling things", and showed people on a mountain top watching as thirty million men throw themselves against each other:

> They seem to see a great livid plain unrolled, which to
> their seeing is made of mud and water, while figures
> appear and fast fix themselves to the surface of it, all
> blinded and borne down with filth, like the dreadful
> castaways of shipwreck. (*Under Fire*, Chapter 1).

He believed that this was a kind of cannibalism — "Two armies fighting each other — that's like one great army committing suicide.... It is we who are the material of war. War is made up of the flesh and the souls of common soldiers only. It is we who make the plains of dead and the rivers of blood, all of us, and each of us is invisible and silent because of the immensity of our numbers" (Chapter 24).

These images lodged in Owen's mind and fused with his memories of "the ground all crawling and wormy with wounded bodies" (Letter 510), the first time he had been in a "show". So he perceives himself, at first a detached spectator, looking down on a vast tract of Europe. The ravaged, diseased land is dominated by trenches and shell-holes, a "beard" of wire, and the moving caterpillars. The grey ones are the Germans, the "brown", presumably, men in khaki. There is no moral difference because all are "migrants from green fields, intent on mire"; they have destroyed nature and turned their backs on normal life in order to fight. Nobody wins; they merely eat and are eaten. The dead plug ditches while the still living vanish down holes; these dug-outs and tunnels were important in his poetry and he comments, here as elsewhere, on their foul smell. As one of the more powerful couplets says, the combatants hardly seem human, just a form of insect life going through a painful and revolting struggle:

> I saw their bitten backs curve, loop and straighten,
> I watched those agonies curl, lift and flatten.

He was now fully in control of the form he would use in 'Strange Meeting'. But at this point, he ceases to be a spectator and we realise his individual agony for the first time. Like the doomed figures of mythology, Lucifer or Icarus, he falls from a great height earthwards. Death shows him a bruised worm, trying to hide from the conflict, "and the fresh-severed head of it, my head". It is a terrifying climax. He had undoubtedly seen severed heads and feet, perhaps had nightmares about them, but there is also the suggestion that he is "a platoon commander lying dead or helpless while his leaderless men find what shelter they can" (DH 135). They have all come to grief in No Man's Land, and it is partly his fault.

Owen's guilt feelings about his 'cowardice', which he could not describe in detail, may explain why this poem is difficult to interpret. But clearly he knew that he could not simply be an observer, like Hardy writing about a war a hundred years earlier. He was deeply involved, and part of the violence himself.

'Exposure', by contrast, gives a worm's-eye view of life on the front line. It is based on Owen's experiences in early 1917, when he and his companions were lying out in the snow. "The marvel is that we did not all die of cold. As a matter of fact, only one of my party actually froze to death before he could be got back.... My feet ached until they could ache no more, and so they temporarily died. I was kept warm by the ardour of Life within me. I forgot hunger in the hunger for Life" (Letter 482).

EXPOSURE

Our brains ache, in the merciless iced east winds that
           knive us...
Wearied we keep awake because the night is silent...
Low, drooping flares confuse our memory of the salient...
Worried by silence, sentries whisper, curious, nervous,
    But nothing happens.

Watching, we hear the mad gusts tugging on the wire,
Like twitching agonies of men among its brambles.
Northward, incessantly, the flickering gunnery rumbles,
Far off, like a dull rumour of some other war.
    What are we doing here?

The poignant misery of dawn begins to grow ....
We only know war lasts, rain soaks, and clouds sag
           stormy.
Dawn massing in the east her melancholy army
Attacks once more in ranks on shivering ranks of grey,
    But nothing happens.

Sudden successive flights of bullets streak the silence.
Less deathly than the air that shudders black with snow,
With sidelong flowing flakes that flock, pause and renew;
We watch them wandering up and down the wind's
           nonchalance,
    But nothing happens.

Pale flakes with fingering stealth come feeling for our
        faces —
We cringe in holes, back on forgotten dreams, and stare,
        snow-dazed,
Deep into grassier ditches. So we drowse, sun-dozed,
Littered with blossoms trickling where the blackbird
        fusses,
  — Is it that we are dying?

Slowly our ghosts drag home: glimpsing the sunk fires,
        glozed
With crusted dark-red jewels; crickets jingle there;
For hours the innocent mice rejoice: the house is theirs;
Shutters and doors, all closed: on us the doors are closed,
  We turn back to our dying.

Since we believe not otherwise can kind fires burn;
Nor ever suns smile true on child, or field, or fruit.
For God's invincible spring our love is made afraid;
Therefore, not loath, we lie out here; therefore were born,
  For love of God seems dying.

Tonight, this frost will fasten on this mud and us,
Shrivelling many hands, puckering foreheads crisp.
The burying-party, picks and shovels in shaking grasp,
Pause over half-known faces. All their eyes are ice,
  But nothing happens.

'Exposure' was once thought to come at the beginning of Owen's great period, but was actually begun in late 1917 and revised at the last opportunity in France in September 1918, and it is mature and brilliant work. There are some daring half-rhymes — "knive us/nervous", "nonchalance/happens" — which come off, as does the short, simple, hanging line at the end of each verse.

"Passive suffering is not a theme for poetry", Yeats wrote in his preface to the *Oxford Book of Modern Verse* (1936), justifying his decision to exclude almost all the war poets. In fact most Owen poems are not about passive suffering, but this one very obviously is; as it says four times, "nothing happens". Nothing, that is, except tiny changes in the time of day, the weather and the war's progress; dawn breaks, there is a flight of bullets, rain turns to snow. The men appear permanently trapped in a state between life and death, and the poem's movement is circular. When it ends they are exactly where they were in the first verse; one night has been lived through, when the next night comes they will still be there; the only change that seems possible is death.

"What are we doing here?" the poet asks. A good question, which he will attempt to answer in his own time. The bullets do less harm than 'exposure' to the climate. Dawn looks like a German army, grey-clad, but the real cause of the men's suffering is lying out in the open under freezing conditions, with some psychological force forbidding them to get up and walk away. The irresistible parallel is with hanging on a cross, and the seventh verse examines the possibility that they are suffering for others.

It has often been noticed that "our brains ache" parodies the opening of Keats' 'Ode to a Nightingale',"My heart aches".Owen was aware that his generation was living through horrors which the Romantics had not dreamed of, and that poetry must change in order to describe them. Half-conscious, he recalls the past and imagines a Romantic or Georgian trench, with sun, grass, and blackbirds, only to see that this is the equivalent of going to sleep in the snow. In the sixth verse they keep themselves going (as he really did) with thoughts of home:

Slowly our ghosts drag home....

It would seem they are ghosts already, on the borderline of life and death. But there is no comfort in the idea that they are defending their homes because these are closed and empty. "Keep the home fires burning", said the Ivor Novello song, "...though your lads are far away they dream of home". But the fires are almost dead. "Crusted dark-red jewels" is an example of the care Owen takes with small phrases; the fires are beautiful, but, like jewels, offer no warmth or comfort. The house has been deserted by its human inhabitants and is left to mice and crickets. It is a haunting picture.

For, the sixth verse strongly suggests, if he and his friends did drag themselves home they would not be welcome. The mice are "innocent", or ignorant, because they live by their instincts and "rejoice" when they are given warmth, shelter and the other blessings of civilisation. They cannot be blamed because those at home have chosen to abandon the house — which represents everything valuable they possessed — and sent the young men away. "Shutters and doors, all closed: on us the doors are closed", the poem laments, with the emphasis on *us*. They are compelled and expected to stay where they are.

The penultimate verse can be read two ways. The obvious meaning is that the soldiers are Christ-figures, dying willingly ("not loath") so that others can live. Owen certainly had some sympathy with this viewpoint, but in other poems he recognised that soldiers were killers as well as victims, and by this time he doubted whether their sacrifice was doing much good. So the words "we believe" must be heavily stressed. He had believed, early in 1917, that they were suffering for a reason, but now he is not prepared to state this categorically. "Love of God seems dying" could mean either that human beings no longer love God (which is why they wage war), or that God no longer loves them (which is why they are in agony). Either way, the simple Christianity he had been taught at home and Dunsden seems inappropriate.

The last verse makes it clear that, since they have been abandoned, the only possible change in their situation is that some of them will die. The next night seems likely to finish them off and he already foresees the arrival of the burying-party, but, at the moment, nothing is still happening. There are few other poems which so convincingly evoke the passing of time.

'Miners', although it does not appear to be about the war, is also concerned with victims:

MINERS

There was a whispering in my hearth,
A sigh of the coal,
Grown wistful of a former earth
It might recall.

I listened for a tale of leaves
And smothered ferns,
Frond-forests, and the low, sly lives
Before the fauns.

My fire might show steam-phantoms simmer
From Time's old cauldron,
Before the birds made nests in summer,
Or men had children.

But the coals were murmuring of their mine,
And moans down there
Of boys that slept wry sleep, and men
Writhing for air.

And I saw white bones in the cinder-shard.
Bones without number;
For many hearts with coal are charred
And few remember.

I thought of all that worked dark pits
Of war, and died
Digging the rock where Death reputes
Peace lies indeed.

Comforted years will sit soft-chaired,
In rooms of amber;
The years will stretch their hands, well-cheered
By our lives' ember.

The centuries will burn rich loads
With which we groaned,
Whose warmth shall lull their dreaming lids,
While songs are crooned;
But they will not dream of us poor lads,
Lost in the ground.

This is thought to have been written in response to the Halmerend pit explosion on 12 January 1918 in which a hundred and forty men and boys were killed, but the poet's interest in miners went back a long way. He had certainly read Wilfrid Gibson's 'Fires' which said the same thing, though less memorably:

Snug in my easy chair,
I stirred the fire to flame ....
Till, dazzled by the drowsy glare,
I shut my eyes to heat and light;

And saw, in sudden night,
Crouched in the dripping dark,
With steaming shoulders stark,
The man who hews the coal to feed my fire.

The sacrifices of miners have struck a deep chord through much of the twentieth century, having been described in countless novels and in poems like Robert Morgan's 'Blood Donor' and Duncan Bush's 'Pneumoconiosis'. Many of the men in Owen's regiment were Lancashire miners and Mary Newboult, in Edinburgh, remembered him discussing their working conditions with great sympathy. So it was not surprising that he should write a poem about the disaster, or that it should get "mixed up with the war at the end" (Blunden 125).

Some people, then and now, drew a distinction between 'unpatriotic' miners and 'brave men in the army', but in this poem their suffering is connected. There is only one direct reference to the war, in verse 6, but Owen noted beside it in his provisional table of contents, 'How the Future will forget the dead in war'.

He imagines himself sitting by the fire, musing on how coal had been formed from ancient forests (with his interest in the earth sciences, he would have long been aware of this) and indulging in the time-honoured game of seeing pictures in the flames. At first he would like to depoliticise the origins of coal. But he sees something more recent and relevant than prehistory, men and boys who have been "smothered" like the ferns and never brought to the surface. "There's blood on the coal" is almost too well-known a metaphor, but what the poet sees is bones, the colour of white ash. They are "without number" because no one is sufficiently concerned to count the bodies. All we know is that, like the victims of the Great War, their numbers are vast. This causes him to remember men who dug trenches and sappers who did perilous work in underground tunnels. "The War was mainly a matter of holes and ditches", as Sassoon said in *Memoirs of an Infantry Officer* (8,5). Tunnels, deep pits, the underworld, these things haunted the poet's imagination and would dominate 'Strange Meeting'. Although he has surfaced (being temporarily out of the war) and can relax beside the fires he had dreamed of in 'Exposure', he cannot forget what it was like to be below ground, or that others are still there. He is conscious, too, that time passes, and that some day the war will be a remote memory. By then he had read Barbusse and perhaps noted

> a Difference which becomes evident between human beings, a Difference far deeper than that of nations and with defensive trenches more impregnable ... between those who gain and those who grieve, those who are required to sacrifice all, *all*, to give their numbers and strength and suffering to the last limit, those upon whom the others walk and advance, smile and succeed. (*Under Fire*, Chapter 22)

The last verses are not bitter; they merely point out that the comfortable tend not to think too much about victims. They are 'lost'; not only are their lives cut short, but their memory has also vanished.

This is one of Owen's few great poems which is not primarily about the war; there is a connection, but conceivably the sixth verse could be left out. Some have found him a limited poet — one biography of Rosenberg states that "Rosenberg was far more than a war poet and Owen was not" (Joseph Cohen, *Journey to the Trenches* [1975], 146) — and many have wondered what he would have written about if he had lived. 'Miners' may suggest an answer. He saw war as only a part of man's inhumanity to man, although for his generation it was of course the most important part. But he was aware that there were other subjects, which he had too little time to explore.

Some time later he wrote his most famous poem, 'Strange Meeting', which, if all his other work had perished, would still have made his reputation. Sassoon called it his "passport to immortality", and recently the *Guardian* named it "the poem of the century". I do not quarrel with this verdict.

STRANGE MEETING

It seemed that out of battle I escaped
Down some profound dull tunnel, long since scooped
Through granites which titanic wars had groined.
Yet also there encumbered sleepers groaned,
Too fast in thought or death to be bestirred.

1. Wilfred as a soldier, aged about 3

2. Wilfred the student at Reading, aged about 19

4. With Laurant Tailhade, France, September 1914

3. At Dunsden Vicarage, early 1912

5. The Owen Family in 1913: Harold, Susan, Colin, Tom, Mary

6. Siegfried Sassoon

7. Wilfred with Arthur Newboult, July 1917

8. Wilfred, the last photograph, late August 1918

9. 'The Canal, Uffington Village' by Harold Owen

10. The Sambre and Oise Canal, November 1918

11. 'The Tiger: "Curious, I seem to hear a child weeping"' Prophetic cartoon by Will Dyson: Clemenceau leaves the Versailles Conference

12. 'Ecstasy of Fumbling' (1991) by Gulf War artist John Keane

Then, as I probed them, one sprang up, and stared
With piteous recognition in fixed eyes,
Lifting distressful hands, as if to bless.
And by his smile, I knew that sullen hall, —
By his dead smile I knew we stood in Hell.

With a thousand pains that vision's face was grained;
Yet no blood reached there from the upper ground,
And no guns thumped, or down the flues made moan.
'Strange friend', I said, 'here is no cause to mourn'.
'None', said that other, 'save the undone years,
The hopelessness. Whatever hope is yours,
Was my life also; I went hunting wild
After the wildest beauty in the world,
Which lies not calm in eyes, or braided hair,
But mocks the steady running of the hour,
And if it grieves, grieves richlier than here.
For by my glee might many men have laughed,
And of my weeping something had been left,
Which must die now. I mean the truth untold,
The pity of war, the pity war distilled.
Now men will go content with what we spoiled,
Or, discontent, boil bloody, and be spilled.
They will be swift with swiftness of the tigress.
None will break ranks, though nations trek from pro
    gress.
Courage was mine, and I had mystery,
Wisdom was mine, and I had mastery:
To miss the march of this retreating world
Into vain citadels that are not walled.
Then, when much blood had clogged their chariot-
    wheels,
I would go up and wash them from sweet wells,
Even with truths that lie too deep for taint.
I would have poured my spirit without stint
But not through wounds; not on the cess of war.
Foreheads of men have bled where no wounds were.

'I am the enemy you killed, my friend.
I knew you in this dark: for so you frowned
Yesterday through me as you jabbed and killed.
I parried; but my hands were loath and cold.
Let us sleep now....'

Other Owen poems, it can be argued, are more perfect. Some lines in the central section seem clotted, such as "I went hunting wild .... richlier than here", or "courage ....mastery", and it is likely that he did not consider the poem finished (the great line, "Let us sleep now", which trails off into silence, may have been added as an afterthought). Yet 'Strange Meeting' remains the great poem of the war, because Owen was not just writing a series of haunting lines but creating a myth. Enemies are reconciled; the dead from both sides rest together but, in the end, can only warn. As was said above, our response is conditioned by the fact that we know he was killed. Early readers believed it to be his last poem, which it was not, but it comes to us like a voice from the grave, warning.

He took the title, probably knowingly, from Shelley. The pacifist hero in *The Revolt of Islam* (1818) single-handedly reconciles two armies with the words:

> O wherefore should ill ever flow from ill,
> And pain still keener pain for ever breed?
> We all are brethren — even the slaves who kill
> For hire, are men; and to avenge misdeed
> On the misdoer, doth but Misery feed.

Like Christ, he is wounded himself but preaches peace:

> And one whose spear had pierced me, leaned beside
> With quivering lips and humid eyes; — and all
> Seemed like some brothers on a journey wide
> Gone forth, whom now strange meeting did befall
> In a strange land
> (Canto Fifth)

Shelley was one influence; another was Dante's *Inferno* (which he had read in translation), where the poet visits hell and meets dead friends. Yet another was Sassoon's 'The Rear-Guard', based on a real experience and a darker poem than Shelley's. A man is groping along a tunnel fifty feet down when he finds a body:

> Tripping, he grabbed the wall; saw someone lie
> Humped at his feet, half-hidden by a rug,
> And stooped to give the sleeper's arm a tug.

> 'I'm looking for headquarters'. No reply.
> 'God blast your neck!' (For days he'd had no sleep,)
> 'Get up and guide me through this stinking place'.
> Savage, he kicked a soft, unanswering heap,
> And flashed his beam across the livid face....

Of course, the man is dead.

By this stage of the war, Owen knew the dark tunnels below and around the battle zone very well. He had also been trapped for three hours in the London underground during an air raid in 1916, "I noticed the passages unduly encumbered, and found the outlet just closed, and Liverpool St. in complete darkness.... There was just room to move from one Exit to another seeking an escape' (Letter 411). The tunnels would have seemed an appropriate place for a dream-like experience.

So he constructed his myth, more intense than any of those which had suggested it. And here we should note the poem's superb sense of drama. As in the film *Incident at Owl Creek*, the speaker does not know at first that he is dead and nor do we. He thinks he has escaped from battle (no hero, this man), but the tunnels are not those of the western front but older ones which have been built for other wars; Owen is putting violence in its historical perspective. Still in the grip of his former habits, he insensitively 'probes' the bodies and is confronted by a Shelley-like figure, "lifting distressful hands as if to bless". Only then does he realise the truth which he has been suppressing:

> By his dead smile I knew we stood in hell.

Not Valhalla, the traditional home of dead warriors, not the Christian heaven which the Church promised soldiers, but hell. The shock of this line, when we read it for the first time, is devastating. By agreeing to take part in the battle, they have damned themselves eternally.

It has been argued that 'the Other' is Owen's, or the speaker's, double. I can see no evidence for this; he does not recognise him, although they will turn out to be intimately connected. But he is a man who could have been his friend, and who is further along the road to wisdom than himself. As he begins to speak, we are reminded that the battle is still going on. The phrases "no blood" and "no guns" make it clear, paradoxically, that blood and guns exist. When the first man says that there is "no cause to mourn", the kind of false comfort which was constantly being given the bereaved, the other insists that death and loss cannot be smoothed away. Owen had already said the same thing in the last lines of 'The End'.

They have both had hopes and ambitions. "The other" had been searching for "the wildest beauty in the world", which "mocks the steady running of the hour", that is, resists time. I take this to mean that he was not concerned with short-term pleasure (running after women?) but wanted to achieve something permanent, whether by writing poetry, or helping his fellow men in some other way. Now these hopes must die. He has a very dark vision of the future; with the best people dead, men will either be content with a damaged post-war world or blunder into new wars:

> They will be swift with swiftness of the tigress,
> None will break ranks, though nations trek from
>   progress.

Possibly he has in mind 'the tiger' Clemenceau, but his main point is that men's talents are misused to make them obedient and efficient killers. They have not broken ranks to stop the present war so why should they do so in future, especially now that those who have learned "the truth untold" are dead? If he and the poet had survived, they might have stopped the world retreating "into vain citadels that are not walled" (offer no real protection). By "vain citadels", Owen meant most of the things that statesmen were and are concerned with — "glory, honour, might, majesty, dominion or power" as the Preface says. After the blood-letting, the world might have been ready to listen to truths which were not poisoned, but it is too late. Certainly Vera Brittain and others believed that the hopeless muddling of the post-war years was because the best of the young men had been killed.

In the closing passage, we get the second and final shock. The other reveals his identity, "I am the enemy you killed, my friend", reminding us of Oscar Wilde's

> Yet each man kills the thing he loves

and of the rejected commandment 'love your enemies'. The line originally read

> I was a German conscript, and your friend

but Owen revised this; he feared that there would be future wars and wanted his poem to be relevant to any time or place. The word "conscript", too, might have sounded patronising, suggesting something like "we are fighting the Kaiser, not poor ignorant German conscripts". Quite possibly the man had gone to war for principled or idealistic reasons, like Wilfred, but in the end they became like Shelley's "slaves who kill". One has stabbed the other, jabbing with a bayonet, and been killed himself the following day. The "I" in this poem is not necessarily Wilfred, but it will be argued in the next chapter that, by depicting himself as a killer, he accepted a measure of guilt. Perhaps the other man's failure to resist effectively — "I parried; but my hands were loath and cold" — was because he had already grown tired of killing; he appears to have more insight than the poet did when he first entered hell. But the understanding dies with him. They are trapped now, and can only sleep.

Another great Ripon poem, which shows Owen working at the height of his powers, is 'The Send-Off':

THE SEND-OFF

Down the close darkening lanes they sang their way
To the siding-shed,
And lined the train with faces grimly gay.

Their breasts were stuck all white with wreath and spray
As men's are, dead.

Dull porters watched them, and a casual tramp
Stood staring hard,
Sorry to miss them from the upland camp.

Then, unmoved, signals nodded, and a lamp
Winked to the guard.

So secretly, like wrongs hushed-up, they went.
They were not ours:
We never heard to which front these were sent;

Nor there if they yet mock what women meant
Who gave them flowers.

Shall they return to beating of great bells
In wild train-loads?
A few, a few, too few for drums and yells,

May creep back, silent, to village wells,
Up half-known roads.

To my mind, this is Owen's most perfect poem; it is quieter-toned than some but makes its point with absolute clarity. The four five-line verses are broken up into groups of three and two lines, continuing his move away from traditional forms.

From the beginning, the atmosphere seems sinister. Although the men are singing and displaying flowers, there are already hints that most of them are going to their deaths. The lanes are darkening; the shed, another dark "close" place, reminds us of execution sheds and slaughter-houses. The ceremonial part of their send-off is over and they are now being packed into trains, watched only by "dull" porters and the uninspiring figure of a tramp. Traditionally flowers have a double significance, coloured for celebration, white for mourning. So the women who stuck flowers on their breasts thought they were expressing support but are actually garlanding them for the slaughter (like the heifer in Keats' 'Ode to a Grecian Urn'). Their departure is like "wrongs hushed-up" because the true nature of what is happening to them is being concealed.

I said earlier that Owen distrusted public emotion — that is, cheering crowds, bells, drums, flags, giving flowers to strangers. His contemporary Pasternak summed this up as "the power of the glittering phrase", and also traced it back to the First World War. "People imagined that it was out of date to follow their own moral sense, that they must all sing the same tune in chorus, and live by other people's notions, the notions which were being crammed down everybody's throat" (*Dr Zhivago*, (1957), 13, 14). The highly-organised displays which have just ended can only obstruct true communication between people, and clear thought.

Of the men who have been sent off, only a few will survive and each of them must find his own way back. The healing process, as Owen had discovered at Craiglockhart, needs silence and privacy. In a letter home, he had described how the Germans "choked up the wells with farmyard refuse" (Letter 499), and the image found its way into two poems, 'Strange Meeting' where the "sweet wells" wash away blood, and this one. Village wells are a traditional meeting-place where travellers can find refreshment, and half-known roads, it is suggested, are better than the broad highway of public opinion. It is a beautiful and impressive statement.

During and after the war, many people could not bear to watch a train moving away, because this reminded them of a last meeting. Today, we think of trains being packed with victims for the concentration camps, other wrongs that were hushed up.

Another short and highly-wrought poem, written the same spring, was one of the few to be published in his lifetime:

FUTILITY

Move him into the sun —
Gently its touch awoke him once,
At home, whispering of fields half-sown.
Always it woke him, even in France,
Until this morning and this snow.
If anything might rouse him now
The kind old sun will know.

Think how it wakes the seeds —
Woke once the clays of a cold star.
Are limbs, so dear achieved, are sides
Full-nerved, still warm, too hard to stir?
Was it for this the clay grew tall?
— O what made fatuous sunbeams toil
To break earth's sleep at all?

It is a snowy morning in the war zone, the sun just risen, and we are looking at the dead body of a young man. Naturally we assume he has been killed by a bullet and this may be the case, as his sides are "still warm". But I see this poem as a sequel to 'Exposure', since we know that the earlier work is based on Owen's experiences in the winter of 1917 when one of his party froze to death. If so, the long agony is over, the men have been relieved and everyone feels better because the sun has come up. A former private wrote about "the sheer ecstasy of the first gleam of sunshine" after a night in the open. "To feel its warmth penetrating one's chilled bones is something beyond my power to describe" (Denis Winter, *Death's Men* [1978], 96). But during the night one man has died of cold, and although he was not directly killed it is still an unnatural death, because he was placed in that situation by the war.

Whether or not this meaning was intended, there is a tragic contrast between the bright sunshine and the body which had been alive until very recently. Morning, especially a sunny morning, is supposed to be a time of hope. Apparently the man had been a farm labourer ("in Wales", says an early draft) and would normally have been getting up at this time to sow the fields. They are now left half-sown, his life over at the halfway mark, and perhaps there is a suggestion that he was too young to sow seed of another kind and has left no descendants. The poet cannot yet accept that he is dead and indulges in the thought that the sun might rouse him. After all, it is the sun which keeps all human life going and, he suggests, long ago it coaxed primitive life-forms from the clay of "a cold star", the earth. Since then we have evolved a long way, yet the sun is helpless against the destructive power of men.

We know that Owen worried about his younger brothers, and also that he had had more to do with caring for children than most men. The second verse expresses what many women feel; why should they spend long years helping their sons grow tall if their lives are going to be ended in a moment? Words like "dear-achieved" and "toil" stress that this is a huge task which does not deserve to be rewarded by premature death. The brightness of the sun seems "fatuous", he concludes, in deep depression, if we are going to defy the creative process and go on killing.

During the summer of 1918, when time was very limited, Owen began a poem which he did not finish to his satisfaction:

THE ROADS ALSO

The roads also have their wistful rest,
When the weather-cocks perch still and roost
And the looks of men turn kind to clocks
And the trams go empty to their drome.
The streets also dream their dream.

The old houses muse of the old days
And their fond trees lean on them and doze.
On their steps chatter and clatter stops
[On their doors a strange hand taps]
For the cries of other times hold men
And they hear the unknown moan.

They remember alien ardours and far futures
And the smiles not seen in happy features.
Their begetters call them from the gutters;
In the gardens unborn child-souls wail,
And the dead scribble on walls.

Though their own child cry for them in tears,
Women weep but hear no sound upstairs.
They believe in love they have not lived
And passion past the reach of stairs
To the world's towers or stars.

"Clearly a Modernist street scene", writes Dominic Hibberd, "in the style of numerous Sitwell poems. It is almost the only clue on which one might base an answer to the frequent question as to what he would have written had he lived" (DH 154). But 'The Roads Also' is just a fragment, though a highly interesting one, and two different versions exist. In the later one Owen dropped the haunting line "On their doors a strange hand taps", and, in verse 3:

As the dusk unearths old mournful odours

which shows that his mind was running on twilight and sadness.
It was a late poem, apparently based on a walk round narrow eighteenth-century streets in Scarborough, at a time of "twilight and the Sunday evening bell" (Letter 592). Some of the old walls

had inscriptions on them, the genesis of the last line in verse 3.

Modernist it certainly is, in the sense that it does not have an obvious 'meaning'. Even if it had been completed, it would have told no story, made no protest, and unsophisticated readers might well have found it trivial. Obviously it does not have the status of his great war poems, but to me and some others, it is fascinating.

Poets in the trenches often thought they were fighting for an idealised, rural England — "her flowers to love, her ways to roam", as Rupert Brooke put it — and many Owen poems, too, draw their images from nature. But the twentieth century saw an enormous shift from a rural to a town-based civilisation, the war speeding up this process. And it had been noted long before, by Wordsworth, that life in cities breaks the links between people:

> How oft, amid those overflowing streets,
> Have I gone forward with the crowd, and said
> Unto myself, 'The face of everyone
> That passes by me is a mystery!'
> *(The Prelude* (1850), vii 626-29).

Owen knew this poem, and had also quite obviously been influenced by the work of the Sitwells and their friends in *Wheels 1917*. This is full of street scenes, their atmosphere sad and sometimes menacing. Osbert's poem 'London' has several lines which echo Owen's (my italics):

> I love the *houses*, russet-brown with smoke...
> *Old* sagging papers from dismantled *walls* ...
> The painted *trams* pass with metallic clatter...

The young poet Iris Tree (1897-1968) has very similar images in her 'In Nassau':

> All down the somnolent *street* where pale tinged
> *houses dream*....
> We have *rest* here and a monotony of wheels....
> But pain comes stabbing in the night ....
> And nothing rids us utterly of grief,
> We who have pilgrim *souls* that will not sleep.

In another poem, 'Myself in the City', she talks about the houses "bent with age ... in a slow decline", and hints at a conflict between mothers and children, "Crab-like the *children* crawled, while always hammering above their heads the scolding shrewish tongue". Another poet, Helen Rootham, writes:

> As some uncared-for, dusty shell
> Still covers, hidden deep,
> The murmur that a *child* once heard,
> So the sad *houses* sleep.
>   ('Cul-de-Sac').

"The roads also have their wistful rest" — the first line of Owen's poem could follow straight on from the last line here. The streets and town houses are not a neutral backdrop but are impregnated with nostalgia. It is evening, the end of the working day, and the poet is dreaming of the old days when everything seemed simpler. The early poems of T.S. Eliot, which also spring from a jaded urban sensibility, come to mind.

The war seemed to have destroyed all tradition, all loving relationships, possibly all hope. Examine the Owen fragment, especially the last two verses, and you find not just a vague Romantic longing but a terrible sadness. Women and their children are both weeping but cannot hear each other; this may hint at the deep division between women and their sons at the front. "Unborn child-souls wail" — these are babies lost at or before birth who traditionally find no home in earth, hell or heaven. In 'Asleep' Owen had referred to "the aborted life ... leaping" within a man who was killed, and in both poems he is mourning for unfulfilled potential. "The dead scribble on walls" surely means not just that there are inscriptions on the walls of old Scarborough, written by the long-dead, but that the more recent dead are around too and trying to pass on messages. Whether we can read 'the writing on the wall' is not clear. To use another modern phrase, the poem is all about alienation.

It is imperfect. "Alien ardours and far futures" is a piece of cloudy, 'poetic' language which means little, and it is not at all clear what the last two lines are about. But there are other lines, particularly those about the unborn children and the dead, which are as memorable as anything Owen wrote. It does suggest that, as Dominic Hibberd says, "he might have helped to bridge the post-war gap between Modernism and the native English tradition".

There was a lull in September 1918 during which Owen was able to write and revise some poems, including 'Smile, Smile, Smile', which, like 'The Roads Also', may be seen by some as untypical work. As in 'The Dead-Beat' and 'The Chances', written a year before, the pity is mixed with a vein of harsh satire:

SMILE, SMILE, SMILE

Head to limp head, the sunk-eyed wounded scanned
Yesterday's *Mail*; the casualties (typed small)
And (large) Vast Booty from our Latest Haul.
Also, they read of Cheap Homes, not yet planned,
'For', said the paper, 'when this war is done
The men's first instincts will be making homes.
Meanwhile their foremost need is aerodromes,
It being certain war has but begun.
Peace would do wrong to our undying dead, —
The sons we offered might regret they died
If we got nothing lasting in their stead.
We must be solidly indemnified.
Though all be worthy Victory which all bought,
We rulers sitting in this ancient spot
Would wrong our very selves if we forgot
The greatest glory will be theirs who fought,
Who kept this nation in integrity'.
Nation? — The half-limbed readers did not chafe
But smiled at one another curiously
Like secret men who know their secret safe.
(This is the thing they know and never speak,
That England one by one had fled to France,
Not many elsewhere now, save under France.)
Pictures of these broad smiles appear each week,
And people in whose voice real feeling rings
Say: How they smile! They're happy now, poor things.

This is very late work, from around 22 September 1918 when Owen wrote to Sassoon, "Did you see what the Minister of Labour said in the *Mail* the other day? "The first instincts of the men *after the cessation of* hostilities will be to return home". And again — "All

classes *acknowledge* their indebtedness to the soldiers & sailors....".
About the same day, Clemenceau is reported by the *Times* as
saying: "*All* are worthy ... yet we should be untrue to ourselves if
we forgot that the *greatest* glory will be to the splendid poilus, who,
etc." (Letter 660). A *poilu* is a French private soldier. The relevant
part of Clemenceau's speech runs:

> All are worthy of victory, because they will know how to
> honour it. Yet, however, in the ancient spot where sit the
> fathers of the Republic we should be untrue to ourselves if
> we forgot that the greatest glory will be to those splendid
> *poilus*.... At the present moment they ask for nothing more
> than to be allowed to complete the great work which will
> assure them of immortality. What do they want and what
> do you? To keep on fighting victoriously until the moment
> when the enemy will understand there is no possible nego-
> tiation between crime and right.

Like Sitwell's 'Armchair', this is a jeering and bitter poem,
savagely parodying ruling-class language and contrasting it with
the fate of their victims. The wounded, sunk-eyed and with
missing limbs, are reading the only kind of papers which they are
allowed to see. By this stage of the war "respect for the truthfulness
of the Press was clean gone" (C.E. Montague, *Disenchantment*
[1922], 193), and Owen shows a keen awareness of the way it
distorts things, saying little about casualties but headlining "Vast
Booty from our Latest Haul". This suggests that "booty" is more
important than lives, and also sets up a crucial distinction between
'us' and 'them'. To any intelligent reader, it is obvious that the men
are being treated with contempt. They are offered cheap homes,
which are unlikely to materialise, while being urged to go on
fighting indefinitely. As always, the dead are used as an argument
against those who want to prevent more killing. "The sons *we*
offered might regret they died / If *we* got nothing lasting in their
stead. / *We* must be solidly indemnified" (my italics). Indemnities
are war damages, and the speaker seems quite willing to exchange
his sons for a lasting, solid profit. In the last part of the speech, "we
rulers" graciously recognise that the men who fought have played
the greatest part in the victory. That is the final insult, since the
rulers have done precisely nothing (sacrificing their sons, Owen

feels, does not count).

Newspaper language, like political speeches, always sounds poor and one-dimensional beside the human reality. What the wounded men have endured can never be measured by those who write articles to keep the public happy. "Smile, smile, smile" is a chorus from a popular marching song, and the wounded are smiling either because they are glad to be out of it, or because they feel they must keep up a cheerful facade for those at home. But, like the men in the last lines of 'Spring Offensive', they do not speak of everything they know.

They have been told that, by fighting, they are preserving "the nation". But the poet feels that anything good in the nation has already gone; England now belongs to the profiteers, politicians and jingoes. This is what he was trying to say in his letter to Sassoon a few weeks earlier, "I'm in hasty retreat towards the Front. Battle is easier here" (Letter 648). The people who were the best part of the nation have been sent to war, and most are now *under* France. Since the newspapers will not speak the truth, and the victims do not speak at all, well-meaning civilians can have no idea of their agony.

This poem, incidentally, gives no support to those who say that Wilfred was non-political, or non-political about everything but the war. It shows him reading the papers avidly and commenting sceptically, and in his last letters he was still arguing with Leslie Gunston about Allied propaganda. It is not of course his best poem, because it was not revised, and because it relies heavily on newspaper reports, which date. But it does show which side of the political divide he stood on — "sympathy for the oppressed always". It also reveals a distinct gift for satire.

Finally, there is 'Spring Offensive', on which he might have done more work if he had lived. Owen had been in the spring offensive of 1917, which ended in his being shell-shocked, and had described his experience in a letter, "The sensations of going over the top are about as exhilarating as those dreams of falling over a precipice.... I woke up without being squashed. Some didn't. There was an extraordinary exultation in the act of slowly walking forward, showing ourselves openly. There was no bugle and no drum .... Then we were caught in a Tornado of Shells" (Letter 510). His memories clearly contributed something to 'Spring Offensive', and this, not 'Strange Meeting', is his last poem; it was begun in the summer of 1918 and sent back to Sassoon from France after being revised. It is even possible that the last lines were added at the beginning of October after he had "entered hell" for the second time.

SPRING OFFENSIVE

Halted against the shade of a last hill
They fed, and eased of pack-loads, were at ease;
And leaning on the nearest chest or knees
Carelessly slept.
           But many there stood still
To face the stark blank sky beyond the ridge,
Knowing their feet had come to the end of the world.

Marvelling they stood, and watched the long grass
    swirled
By the May breeze, murmurous with wasp and midge;
And though the summer oozed into their veins
Like an injected drug for their bodies' pains,
Sharp on their souls hung the imminent ridge of grass,
Fearfully flashed the sky's mysterious glass.

Hour after hour they ponder the warm field
And the far valley behind, where buttercups
Had blessed with gold their slow boots coming up;
When even the little brambles would not yield
But clutched and clung to them like sorrowing arms.
They breathe like trees unstirred.

Till like a cold gust thrills the little word
At which each body and its soul begird
And tighten them for battle. No alarms
Of bugles, no high flags, no clamorous haste, —
Only a lift and flare of eyes that faced
The sun, like a friend with whom their love is done.
O larger shone that smile against the sun, —
Mightier than his whose bounty these have spurned.

So, soon they topped the hill, and raced together
Over an open stretch of herb and heather

111

Exposed. And instantly the whole sky burned
With fury against them; earth set sudden cups
In thousands for their blood; and the green slope
Chasmed and deepened sheer to infinite space.

Of them who running on that last high place
Breasted the surf of bullets, or went up
On the hot blast and fury of hell's upsurge,
Or plunged and fell away past this world's verge,
Some say God caught them even before they fell.

But what say such as from existence' brink
Ventured but drave too swift to sink,
The few who rushed in the body to enter hell,
And there out-fiending all its fiends and flames
With superhuman inhumanities,
Long-famous glories, immemorial shames —
And crawling slowly back, have by degrees
Regained cool peaceful air in wonder —
Why speak not they of comrades that went under?

We should not think of this as a realistic poem. Owen has set his going-over-the-top experience in a gentle Shropshire landscape, as different as possible from the hideous plains of mud and water in northern France. The buttercups were based on a memory of Uffington, and indeed the dates make it clear that he could not have seen them while in combat. Although some plant life, including the famous poppies, survived on the battlefields, there could hardly have been great quantities of "long grass", or "herb and heather" after prolonged shelling. On the other hand, many of the fiercest battles of the war were attempts to capture hills. In his mind these merged with the hills around Shrewsbury and the "high places" associated with human sacrifice.

He is writing at the height of his powers. The men walk through a flowering, friendly landscape to the "last hill" where they know that many of them are going to be killed. They rest, but it is impossible to forget, and the image of an "injected drug" suggests that they are being artificially stimulated to perform acts which are against nature. In the Great War, men were given rum before going over the top; on the way to the Falklands, they were shown pornographic films. There must be some attempt to take their minds off what is going to happen, and the strain of waiting is very painfully conveyed. After this image comes the great couplet

> Sharp on their souls hung the imminent ridge of grass,
> Fearfully flashed the sky's mysterious glass.

As they look at the hill they are about to storm, the "blank" sky above it is like a fortune-teller's glass reflecting the question in each mind, will I survive? It is more subtle and profound than 'The Chances', but the subject-matter is much the same. When the officer gives the "little word" or order to attack they know exactly what they are doing, and are not happy, but go into battle nonetheless. Their experiences are indescribable; some die, others are "too swift to sink" and come back to normality, but with memories that will be with them for life.

This is the outline of the poem. For its deeper meaning, we need to remember the myth of Antaeus, destroyed when his feet lost contact with the earth. We are to think of them as leaping over a cliff or across a chasm; some return to earth unscathed, others don't. That is the significance of the second verse, where the "warm field", the buttercups, and the little brambles which

> clutched and clung to them like sorrowing arms

— ("hands" in some versions) are attempting to protect them. Deliberately, they turn their backs on all this:

> O larger shone that smile against the sun, -
> Mightier than his whose bounty these have spurned.

The sympathy, the identification with the men is enormous, but the poet's judgment (from which he does not exclude himself) is that they have knowingly rejected the sun, the source of life, and therefore, as in 'Futility', it cannot help them. Once the attack is launched, they are no longer in harmony with nature and it turns "against them". Instead of buttercups smearing their feet with gold, another kind of cup — shell holes — swallows their blood. We do not see a human enemy but a storm of bullets, far more deadly than the relatively harmless wasps in the first verse. The line

> Some say God caught them even before they fell

is certainly not meant as pious consolation. Possibly it would have been changed if Owen had had more time to work on this poem, but he did not. As it is, the words "some say", and then "but what say...?" must be heavily stressed.

Apparently, the answer to this question is "nothing"; some people talk clichés about a holy war but those who have been lifted bodily off the earth by the war giant find the experience very hard to describe. Some have died, like Antaeus, and cannot be spoken of; the rest are stunned and can only crawl back to nature — "cool peaceful air" — to be healed. Desmond Graham suggests that "they do not speak of them because they remind them of what they as killers had brought about. What the soldiers want, is to forget" (*The Truth of War*, 77).

This poem certainly communicates the "extraordinary exultation" of having gone over the top and survived, and, like all those who had done so, Owen felt set apart permanently from those who had not. But, as the last line hints, no one can keep on spurning the bounty of nature for ever. The poem is a warning.

3. Breaking Ranks

"By separating him from the rest of us I found I was beginning to distort the picture", Harold Owen said (JFO III, ix) about his attempts to write a conventional biography of his brother. This final chapter looks at how it is possible to relate Wilfred Owen to some of the great issues of our time. Like it or not, he cannot be separated from the rest of us, because he is now generally agreed to be the great war poet and the century since his birth has been dominated by war.

Just as he made a cult of Keats, others have made a cult of him. This has happened to many other poets who died young — Chatterton, Shelley, Rupert Brooke, Sylvia Plath. Those who knew him had their own fixed image; Susan, for instance, who coped with bereavement by doing everything possible to promote his work:

> I knew without doubt (writes Harold) that the real Wilfred had diverged very far from my mother's conception of *her* Wilfred.... She had built for herself an inviolable image — an image not only in the likeness of what she thought he was but one which she in her simple way so passionately wished him to be. (JFO III, 249)

Harold found the same problem when he met Sassoon after the war, "All that he wanted was to keep his own memory of Wilfred for himself, uninvolved. This deep-rooted dislike of sharing Wilfred was mutual" (*Aftermath* (1970), 17). In the thirties, each believing that he knew Wilfred better than the other, they would clash sharply over whether he would have become a Communist. Meanwhile, in mid-1920s Cambridge, Christopher Isherwood and his friends had made him an icon:

> We claimed the support of the ghosts of our favourite
> writers, particularly of Wilfred Owen, Katherine Mansfield
> and Emily Bronte.... We talked about them as if they were
> our personal friends, wondered what they would have said
> on certain occasions, how they would have behaved, what
> advice they would have given us. One thing we never for
> a moment doubted: that they would have loathed Cam-
> bridge and all its works. (*Lions and Shadows* [1938], 72).

('The real Wilfred', incidentally, would have given years of his life
to get to Cambridge). Later, in the 1926 General Strike, Isherwood
agonised about which side to take. Wilfred, he recalled, had not
"tried vainly to pretend that as an intellectual he belonged to some
mystical Third Estate, isolated above the battle" (180). But Wilfred
gave him no advice and he decided to blackleg.

Another young man who had lost his father in the war was Patric
Dickinson, who as poetry editor for the Third Programme would
do much to publicise Owen's work. Discovering him in the 1930s,
he developed a strong personal feeling for him:

> it was as if an unknown hawk-moth, a creature of beauty
> and of powerful flight had flown by choice into the furnace
> of evil and in its own immolation extinguished the flames
> but left a flameless and inextinguishable radiance — a light
> to see by, such as I had never known before or have known
> since, an inward light to read by, reason and understand....
> Owen was dead, killed, when the war was within seven
> days and seven nights of silence. I thought of that one week,
> I have often thought of it. Seven less days of cold November
> suns, he would have lived. Of all the myriads of men no
> sun could wake, I asked for two. I knew, as I had these
> thoughts, the enormity of their selfishness. I asked forgive-
> ness of the dead, but there was the thought which could not
> be gainsaid. I wanted my father and I wanted Wilfred Owen
> to have lived. (*The Good Minute* [1965], 119)

In 1939, when a great many people had to rethink their pacifism,
he asked himself if he was 'betraying Owen' by consenting to fight.
"I have found many letters lately of Wilfred Owen's", wrote a

friend of Sitwell's (probably Sassoon) around 1950, "and looking back over the time since the last war, I see how much easier all our lives would have been if he had lived" (*Noble Essences*, Chapter 4). Among those who did and did not know him, grief for his death remained intense, as did curiosity about what he would have written, given time. But he himself always wished to direct our attention to the wider questions.

Wilfred Owen's photographs

The legend of Wilfred Owen's war photographs, which has inspired at least one poem, derives from the memories of the librarian Frank Nicholson. He remembered that Wilfred just hinted at "the horrors he had seen and heard of at the Front":

> He did not enlarge upon them, but they were obviously always in his thoughts, and he wished that an obtuse world should be made sensible of them. With this object he was collecting a set of photographs exhibiting the ravages of war upon the men who took part in it — mutilations, wounds, surgical operations and the like. He had some of these photographs with him, and I remember that he put his hand to his breast-pocket to show me them, but suddenly thought better of it and refrained. (Blunden, 134).

The poem is Ted Hughes' 'Wilfred Owen's Photographs', written in the 1950s. It is puzzling at first sight because it says nothing about Owen or photographs, just describes how a group of MPs, in the nineteenth century, try to stop the Navy flogging men with the cat-o'-nine-tails. Reactionaries protest that this is a great national tradition. Then someone brings a 'cat' into the House and the lawmakers feel its bloodstained thongs:

> Whereupon ....
> quietly, unopposed,
> The motion was passed.

The point, for those who know the 'photographs' story, is that many people (especially politicians, perhaps) have to actually see pain and suffering before they react against it. If they merely know about it in the abstract, they will push it to a dark corner of their minds.

The problem is that the story is almost certainly not true. It will be noted that neither Frank Nicholson, nor anyone else, claimed to have actually seen Wilfred's photographs, nor were any found among his things after his death. (He cut out and kept a newspaper photograph showing a muddy plain in France, but that, I will argue, would have changed very few minds). The mystery deepens when we find that Sitwell tells exactly the same story about Robert Ross. Is it possible that both men carried a set of war photographs?

Almost certainly not, because photography was a distinctly minor art at that time. This was not an age when everyone took his camera everywhere, and Wilfred certainly did not take one to the western front. War correspondents were kept away until May 1915 because that made it easier to control information and there was little war photography until the following year. "A camera out here is a phenomenon and a reminder of home which any men anywhere would greet with cheers", wrote Max Plowman (*A Subaltern on the Somme* [1927], 130) — which may explain all those smiling faces in group photographs from the Great War. Studying these photographs, we find surprisingly little that is really shocking. There are fields of mire, mutilated trees, duckboards, ample evidence of what the war had done to the landscape but little about its effect on the human body. Even wounded men had to be portrayed smiling broadly, as in a photograph of September 1918 which Wilfred may have seen. Dead Germans were occasionally shown, in black and white of course and at a distance, but not dead Englishmen. After the war the most upsetting photographs were quietly removed from the archives and they are not often seen even now.

Instead, the papers offered artists' impressions of 'heroic deeds' they had read about. The Royal Academy from 1915 onwards was dominated by war paintings, but, according to Reginald Pound, "the note of truth.... proved elusive. No easels had been set up on the battlefield or on the decks of warships", (*The Lost Generation* [1964], 157). Sassoon observed:

I opened one of the illustrated weeklies and soon found an

article on 'War Pictures at the Royal Academy'. After a panegyric about 'Forward the Guns!' (a patriotic master-piece by a lady who had been to the Military Tournament in pre-War days) the following sentence occurred: "I think I like Mr Blank's 'Contalmaison' picture best. He almost makes one feel that he must have been there. The Nth Division are going over the second line I expect — the tips of their bayonets give one this impression — and it is a picture which makes one's pulse beat a lot faster...." (*Memoirs of an Infantry Officer*, 9, 3).

Wilfred visited the Royal Academy Summer Exhibition of 1917, where many such pictures were on show, but was not impressed.

In 1916 came the official war artists' scheme. As a result,many fine painters (some of them in uniform) were allowed to go to the front and paint what they saw, and British wars have had their official artists ever since. Comparing one genre with another, we find contrasts as deep as that between, say, Rupert Brooke and Wilfred Owen. For instance, 'The Somme Battlefield' by a Miss Oliver, who presumably had not been there, shows a dreamy, Impressionist landscape covered with poppies and a few white crosses, with larks singing in the sky. She must have thought these famous symbols were all that was needed to evoke the right response, and her work could not be more different from the hideous, twisted landscape of Paul Nash's 'The Menin Road'. This has fields of mud where the tiny human figures might drown, shellbursts and searchlights which might kill them; yet, we realise, men have made this mess.

It was pointed out at the time that these pictures could contribute little or nothing to war propaganda. The artists were part of the official war effort, but (like John Keane with his daring 'Mickey Mouse in the Gulf') they often produced something other than what was wanted. William Orpen, in 'Dead Germans in a Trench', shows a grey-faced corpse staring accusingly at the viewer. Paul Nash, in 'We are Making a New World', has the sun rising above the ruins of Delville Wood, scene of constant killing throughout 1916. It is a wilderness of shell holes with no green things or solid ground left; as in 'Futility', the traditional symbol of hope seems pointless. "No pen or drawing can convey this country", Nash wrote home in 1917, unconsciously echoing Owen:

Sunset and sunrise are blasphemous, they are mockeries to man.... It is unspeakable, godless, hopeless. I am no longer an artist interested and curious, I am a messenger who will bring back word from the men who are fighting to those who want the war to go on for ever. Feeble, inarticulate, will be my message, but it will have a bitter truth, and may it burn their lousy souls. (Quoted in Arthur Marwick, *The Deluge* [1965], 238).

One rule was that British corpses should not be painted. In 1918 C.R.W. Nevinson's 'Paths of Glory' had to be withdrawn from exhibition because it showed men on the wire.

We may now, perhaps, glimpse what was in Owen's mind. He described his poem 'A Terre', as "a 'photographic repre-sentation'of an officer dying of wounds" (Letter 609), and perhaps what he told Nicholson was that he was working on a series of "photographic" studies of "the ravages of war upon the men who took part in it" that is, gas injuries, amputations, breakdown, suicide. Ross, who had friends in high places, may really have got hold of some photographs, but Wilfred did not know him at this time and was planning a protest through another medium. Unlike Nash, he could only paint in words and it was to his advantage that most people then got their knowledge of the world through the printed page. So he did everything in his power to make the reader see what he had seen. That accounts for the highly visual quality of some poems and the repeated demand that readers should use their imaginations, "If ... you too could pace ... and watch ... if you could hear" ('Dulce et Decorum Est').

He could not have foreseen how the art of photography would develop. Throughout the century, visual art became less and less representational, so that one of the greatest of all war paintings, Picasso's 'Guernica', makes absolutely no attempt to be 'realistic'. The same is true of the Gulf War pictures of John Keane. At the same time, photography and film made enormous strides and are now recognised as major propaganda weapons. In World War I, the public was shielded from what was happening and the men themselves colluded in this, believing that their families must not be upset. In Vietnam fifty years later it was possible to watch parts of the action in glorious technicolour, with men under bombardment being asked "Do you think it's worth it?" The result was that Americans got tired of the war after much lower casualties than the British had suffered in 1914-18. In the rest of the world, two black and white photographs had the greatest impact. One was of a burning child running along a road (this got into the work of at least two 'Vietnam' poets, suggesting that the photograph is now more powerful than the poem). The other, which will never be forgotten by anyone who saw it, was of a young man about to be shot through the head. The war was eventually stopped in part because of constant bad publicity.

Governments know and fear the power of the visual image. Photographs, moving or static, of starving Africans or homeless Kurds break down barriers of race and culture and cause people to cry out that 'something must be done'. The day after the raid on Libya in 1986, Kate Adie went round filming wounded children and talking to articulate, English-speaking people who described their experience of being bombed. As a result, the public turned against the raid but government ministers were outraged, because her actions humanised the enemy.

By the time of the second Gulf War, in 1991, the planners had learned the lessons of Vietnam and photographers were kept under very tight control. TV viewers saw endless images of men in uniform, tanks, sand, camels and 'smart' bombs which were supposed to hit only military targets. The war became a glorified video game for those at home, as was often said at the time, and the massacre of civilians and young conscripts was carefully concealed from those who might have had qualms. Some subversive photographs did get out when a Baghdad shelter was bombed, killing large numbers of children, but viewers were told that the worst of these were 'too horrifying to show'. That raises the question, why are we not allowed to see what is being done in our name? There were also those who said that it was wrong to show them, because obviously it undermines the war effort if you arouse sympathy for the other side.

Ted Hughes, whose attitudes have been partly formed by his father's memories of the Great War, writes, "The story of Wilfred Owen's 'discovery' of the propaganda power of some photographs is well known. His feeling for the totally new calamity of the trenches, and his inexpressible, raging need to communicate it to what he saw as domestic England's old-fashioned inability to imagine it, was not that far from the environmentalist's position between the injured Earth on one hand and Government, industry and certain fixed ways of life on the other. It prompted him to collect photographs of the trench horrors with the intention of setting them up on public display in London. Frustrated in that, he shifted the compulsion sideways, which helps to explain the precisely angled motive behind the dramatic focus of his poems. But his idea about photographs, obviously, was a true inspiration. Photographs of that suffering, he believed, would force people to imagine it and therefore to feel it, to feel it and therefore to do something about it. To realise how right he was one only has to recall the effect on the course of the Gulf War of two photographs: the rocket-blasted shelter in Baghdad, and the soldier's charred head sticking from the window of the wrecked bus on the road from Basrah" (*Observer*, 29 November 1992).

That photograph (banned in the United States as "too graphically violent"), became the subject of Tony Harrison's 'A Cold Coming', which was published soon afterwards in a national newspaper and so reached a much larger audience than most poems do. It belongs to a long tradition of poetry in which the dead are made to speak, and was immediately compared with Owen's 'Strange Meeting'.

Finally, we should note that war photographers are sometimes killed. When Wilfred went back to the war zone, knowing that was a possibility, he would certainly have hoped to get other "photographic representations", that is, poems.

Not about Heroes: W.B. Yeats

The reaction to the Great War, as I said in Chapter 2, was delayed for several years. Men and women came back to normality, wanting only to forget, and found that the new world they had been promised was mean, shoddy and unwelcoming. Wilfred's brother, who spent most of the 1920s unemployed or in dead-end jobs, wrote of his reference to "the very strange look on all faces" in France, "an incomprehensible look, which a man will never see in England ... a blindfold look, and without expression, like a dead rabbit's" (Letter 578). "Had he survived the war", Harold commented, "he would have seen them all over England in the twenties" (*Aftermath*, 84). Vera Brittain wrote:

'You threw four years into the melting-pot —
Did you indeed!' these others cry. 'Oh well,
The more fool you!'
And we're beginning to agree with them.
('The Lament of the Demobilised')

Ezra Pound summed up the whole experience, in 1920, in a poem which turned its back decisively on Romantic melodies:

Died some, pro patria,
non 'dulce', non 'et decor'....
walked eye-deep in hell
believing in old men's lies....

There died a myriad,
And of the best, among them,
For an old bitch gone in the teeth,
For a botched civilisation....
('Hugh Selwyn Mauberley').

Disgust remained unspoken for the next ten years or so and then found expression in a flood of war books, many of them classics. The best-known autobiographies were Blunden's *Undertones of War* (1928), Sassoon's *Memoirs of a Fox-Hunting Man* (1928) and its sequels, Graves' *Goodbye to All That* (1929) and Vera Brittain's *Testament of Youth*, which she did not publish until 1933 because she realised that no one had yet described the women's war. R.C. Sherriff's play *Journey's End*, set in the dreadful days of March 1918, became a popular hit after its first performance in 1928. Novels included Ford Madox Ford's *Parade's End* (1924-8), Richard Aldington's *Death of a Hero* (1929), Frederic Manning's *Her Privates We*, also known as *The Middle Parts of Fortune*, and Henry Williamson's *Patriot's Progress* (both 1930). From Germany came Erich Maria Remarque's *All Quiet on the Western Front* and from the United States Hemingway's *A Farewell to Arms* (both 1929). These two novels were made into popular films, to be joined in 1937 by the French *La Grande Illusion* which carried the same message about the pointlessness of war. Also in 1937 appeared David Jones' *In Parenthesis*, whose reputation has been slowly growing ever since.

Most of these works dealt with the underside of war — lice, foul language, brothels, VD, the murder of prisoners, 'heroes' desperate to get away and despicable jingoes. One subject which became extraordinarily prominent was that of the man shot, 'at dawn', by his own side for cowardice or desertion. Barbusse touched on it in *Le Feu* and it is a central theme in A.P. Herbert's *The Secret Battle* (1919), C.E. Montague's *Rough Justice* (1926), Arnold Zweig's *The Case of Sergeant Grischa* (1928), Lewis Grassic Gibbon's *Sunset Song* (1932) and Humphrey Cobb's *Paths of Glory* (1935), which became an outstanding film. Orpen sketched the condemned man and he was the subject of poems by Kipling and Herbert Read. A great number of writers spoke more briefly about executions, including Rosenberg with his rat. The hero of *A Farewell to Arms* just escapes being shot by his allies and after that decides to turn his back on the war. (This novel, which had a vast female readership, shows how the cult of God, king and country was giving way to the cult of private life, true love, doing your own thing). The actual number of executions (346 British) was a minute fraction of those who died, so why did they attract such immense attention?

The reason must have been that they summed up the irony of this war in the cruellest possible way. Men had volunteered to fight for their country, and it first drove them to breaking point and then killed them. Death sentences were commuted, more often than not, but they were regularly read out on parade and "filled most hearts with hatred for a system so brutally disposed towards the victims of unprecedented stress" (*The Lost Generation*, 112). The more sensitive, like Graves, got out of sitting on tribunals and dreaded the order to execute a disgraced comrade. One officer, Ralph Partridge, was so distressed by having to command a firing squad that he became a pacifist after the war. By the time Grassic Gibbon wrote *Sunset Song*, which records the war's impact on the land and people of Scotland, the climate of opinion had changed so much that the best man in the book is a conscientious objector. The man who joins the army is brutalised by military life and only redeems himself when he decides to go home, knowing he will be caught and shot. This does not mean that everyone had changed their minds but writers, conscious that they had at first supported the war unquestioningly, and those too young to be involved, had grown cynical.

The time was ripe for the new (1931) edition of Owen's poems which brought him many more admirers. Like the writers already quoted, he gave the disillusioned view, saying that his book was "not about heroes". He did not mention executions (although he joked [Letter 649] that he might be shot if the authorities heard him talk in his sleep), but he did show a compassionate interest in the unheroic aspects of war. 'Mental Cases' describes men whose personalities have been destroyed and who sit in the darkness, rocking themselves and slobbering. 'S.I.W.' (self-inflicted wounds) studies a kind of man who was almost as much despised as the deserter, one who turns his weapon on himself:

> His eyes grew old with wincing, and his hand
> Reckless with ague. Courage leaked, as sand
> From the best sandbags after years of rain.
> But never leave, wound, fever, trench-foot, shock,
> Untrapped the wretch. And death seemed still withheld
> For torture of lying machinally shelled,
> At the pleasure of this world's Powers who'd run amok.
>
> He'd seen men shoot their hands, on night patrol.
> Their people never knew. Yet they were vile.
> 'Death sooner than dishonour, that's the style!'
> So Father said.

In the end he commits suicide. There is no suggestion that he acted weakly or wrongly, rather that even the best men can come to this just as the best sandbags eventually give way. The poem appears to take the view that any man would get out of the trenches if he could, and his father's heroic cliches sound hollow, compared to the reality of slow torture. We have noted that 'Dulce et Decorum Est' and 'Disabled' also show men in extreme states of helplessness.

So, even before the boom in Owen studies, a great many readers agreed with his version of the war and admired him. "Looking back", wrote Orwell, "I think it might have been better for the human race if the authorities had seen fit to exempt Wilfred Owen and conscript Horatio Bottomley" (*Manchester Evening News*, 21

December 1944). But one who did not was W.B. Yeats, who came under fire for excluding him from the 1936 anthology of modern verse which he edited. He wrote in the introduction:

> I have a distaste for certain poems written in the midst of the great war.... I have rejected these poems for the same reason that made Arnold withdraw his 'Empedocles on Etna' from circulation; passive suffering is not a theme for poetry. In all the great tragedies, tragedy is a joy to the man who dies; in Greece the tragic chorus danced.... If war is necessary, or necessary in our time and place, it is best to forget its suffering as we do the discomfort of fever, remembering our comfort at midnight when our temperature fell, or as we forget the worst moments of more painful disease.

The relationship between these two great poets was sadly one-sided. Owen in his last years admired Yeats; his 'Six o'clock in Princes Street' is clearly influenced by 'When you are old', and he used short Yeats quotations to introduce two poems, 'S.I.W.' and 'The Show'. He also hoped to send him a copy of his projected book.

Yeats, on the other hand, had read Owen but had not been impressed. He revealed his real view of him in private:

> When I excluded Wilfred Owen, whom I consider unworthy of the poets' corner of a country newspaper, I did not know I was excluding a revered sandwich-board man of the revolution, and that somebody has put his worst and most famous poem in a glass-case in the British Museum — however, if I had known it, I would have excluded him just the same. He is all blood, dirt and sucked sugar-stick (look at the selection in Faber's Anthology — he calls poets 'bards', a girl a 'maid', and talks about 'Titanic wars'). There is every excuse for him, but none for those who like him. (Letter to Dorothy Wellesley, 21 December 1936).

Partly this was hostility to the young 'pylon poets' who were looking to Owen instead of him for inspiration (in another letter he complained, McCarthy-like, that such poets were Communists). The words "maid" and "bards" come from an immature poem, 'From my Diary, July 1914', which Owen would probably not have published. "Titanic" (used in 'The End' and 'Strange Meeting') does belong to his mature style, and it is hard to see any objection to it. Like the ill-fated ship which had gone down in 1912 (and therefore carrying associations of doom) it means massive, gigantic, something on a non-human scale. This seems perfectly appropriate for describing the first modern war.

The charge that certain Owen poems resemble "sucked sugar-stick" (are unhealthily sweet) is partly true, and will be examined below. The real problem, though, was the dirt and blood.

It is not quite true that Yeats excluded all poems "written in the midst of the great war". He did include 'Into Battle', by Julian Grenfell (died of wounds 1915), a regular army officer and a man who would probably have had trouble fitting into any peaceful society. 'Into Battle', his one major poem, is at the same time impressive and frightening. Like his letters home, it makes it clear that he loved war, "only joy of battle takes/ Him by the throat and makes him blind":

> The naked earth is warm with spring,
> And with green grass and bursting trees
> Leans to the sun's gaze glorying,
> And quivers in the sunny breeze;
> And life is colour and warmth and light,
> And a striving evermore for these;
> And he is dead who will not fight;
> And who dies fighting has increase.
>
> The fighting man shall from the sun
> Take warmth, and life from the glowing earth;
> Speed with the light-foot winds to run,
> And with the trees to newer birth;
> And find, when fighting shall be done,
> Great rest, and fullness after dearth.

Notice the high concentration of traditional images — spring, grass, trees, sun; there is no blood and dirt here. The other images which build up the idea of war as life-enhancing are stars, birds and, particularly, horses:

> In dreary, doubtful, waiting hours,
> Before the brazen frenzy starts,

> The horses show him nobler powers;
> O patient eyes, courageous hearts!

The horses summon up an archaic vision of knights riding into combat on their chargers; in fact they lost their importance as fighting animals soon after 1914. This then is the kind of war poem Yeats liked, the kind which sees war as a joyous and manly adventure. His own poetry is instructive too.

As an Irishman, well over military age, Yeats was about as detached from the war as it was possible to be. On being asked to write something for the war effort he responded with a poem about not writing poetry:

> I think it better that in times like these
> A poet keep his mouth shut.

Yeats was no friend of the British Empire, and the Easter Rising of 1916, its suppression, and the executions which followed (some of men he knew) made him even more disinclined to support Britain's war. Yet he could not condemn it on humanitarian grounds, like Sassoon and Owen, because the ideal of heroism made a powerful appeal to him. 'An Irish Airman Foresees his Death' is an elegy for a friend's son who had volunteered and was shot down over Italy in 1918:

> I know that I shall meet my fate
> Somewhere among the clouds above;
> Those that I fight I do not hate,
> Those that I guard I do not love;
> My country is Kiltartan Cross,
> My countrymen Kiltartan's poor,
> No likely end could bring them loss
> Or leave them happier than before.
> Nor law, nor duty bade me fight,
> Nor public men, nor cheering crowds,
> A lonely impulse of delight
> Drove to this tumult in the clouds;
> I balanced all, brought all to mind,
> The years to come seemed waste of breath,
> A waste of breath the years behind
> In balance with this life, this death.

According to Yeats (we have no way of knowing his real opinions) the airman is not fighting for king and country; he is careful to point out that he comes from a different background and that public patriotism does not move him. He is acting on "a lonely impulse of delight", following his star, doing what turns him on. Like heroes throughout the ages (coincidentally like Rupert Brooke and the rest, but for his own reasons) he has chosen to lead a brief and glorious life instead of a long and dull one, and this is an attitude which the poet admires. He is above ordinary humanity, alone in the clouds, cut off from emotion, blood and dirt. The only kind of war poem Yeats felt able to write was one about a gallant duel with death.

His own country roused stronger emotions. In 'September 1913' he had lamented that "romantic Ireland's dead and gone"; there were no longer any heroes. But in 'Easter 1916' he describes how the rising against British rule changed everything. Ordinary men who worked at counters or desks have become heroes; "a terrible beauty is born". Terrible, because he regrets that they died, and is not convinced it was necessary, but nevertheless his imagination responds to their great gesture. In 'The Rose Tree' he has two leaders of the Rising conclude that they can only win victory for their cause by dying:

> 'But where can we draw water',
> Said Pearse to Connolly,
> 'When all the wells are parched away?
> O plain as plain can be
> There's nothing but our own red blood
> Can make a right Rose Tree'.

There is the same blood imagery in his play *Cathleen ni Hoolihan* (1902). The "old woman" who represents Ireland says, "It is a hard service they take that help me. Many that are red-cheeked now will be pale-cheeked.... They that had red cheeks will have pale cheeks for my sake, and for all that they will think they are well paid". Yeats was a humane man who was repelled by violence when he came in contact with it, and his nationalism was certainly no worse than the British variety. Nevertheless, we can see he was attracted by the idea that men should spill their blood.

With this in mind, we turn to Owen's 'Inspection', a short and underrated poem which may well have been in Yeats's mind when he complained about blood and dirt:

> 'You! What d'you mean by this?' I rapped.
> 'You dare come on parade like this?'
> 'Please, sir, it's —' 'Old yer mouth', the sergeant
>   snapped.
> 'I takes 'is name, sir?' — 'Please, and then dismiss'.
>
> Some days 'confined to camp' he got,
> For being 'dirty on parade'.
> He told me, afterwards, the damnèd spot
> Was blood, his own. 'Well, blood is dirt', I said.
>
> 'Blood's dirt', he laughed, looking away,
> Far off to where his wound had bled
> And almost merged for ever into clay.
> 'The world is washing out its stains', he said.
> 'It doesn't like our cheeks so red:
> Young blood's its great objection.
> But when we're duly white-washed, being dead,
> The race will bear Field Marshal God's inspection'.

The first six lines are a brilliant little sketch of army life outside the battle zone. There is bullying, heavy and unjust punishment, a strict pecking order in which the officer through the NCO imposes his will on the men, who have no rights. It is all a long way from the concept of the officer as father-figure, which Wilfred certainly tried to be. But it is accurate; Rosenberg was punished frequently and one officer refused to let him include poems in his letters because it was a bore to censure them. The atmosphere shocked many men who were quite willing to die for their country but had not expected petty persecution. To keep them disciplined when not fighting, great emphasis was placed on keeping oneself and one's equipment clean, going on parade looking immaculate, whitewashing buildings before they were inspected and so on. A large part of a soldier's life was (is?) consumed by this.

Having punctured a myth or two, the poem moves on to another level. The "damnèd spot" is a very well-known quotation from Shakespeare. "Out damned spot!" says Lady Macbeth, trying to wash her hands (like Pilate) because she knows that she has committed murder and cannot get away from the idea of blood. This warns us that Owen's poem is not a simple satire, but is going to comment on the nature of war. The young man tells the officer that the spot which defiled his clean uniform was his own blood, presumably from an old wound, although they are now far enough behind the lines to concentrate on matters like parades and punishments. By this time the officer is prepared to talk but not to back down:

'Well, blood is dirt', I said.

The "well" suggests that he is having second thoughts, but still cannot accept excuses for the crime of not looking spotless when the army is showing its best face to the world. In the last section the poem abandons colloquial speech. The young man's wound has "almost merged forever into clay", which means that he almost died; clay is not only the earth which receives blood but is also a word used by poets for the human body after death — "was it for this the clay grew tall?" "The world is washing out its stains" — the war is still going on. Someone somewhere does not want young people to live, laugh and be healthy, and the officer and sergeant are the representatives of this impersonal force. Perhaps they will eventually all be killed and then, when there is no young blood anywhere, they can be tidily shut away in graves (whited sepulchres?) and praised. While they are alive God, the world and the army seem determined to torment them.

There is a similar theme in 'Arms and the Boy', which Owen planned to put in his book under the heading "protest — the unnaturalness of weapons". The title is a parody of "arms and the man", a phrase first used by Virgil and the name of an anti-heroic play by Bernard Shaw. This describes how boys are seduced by the glamour of weapons:

Let the boy try along this bayonet-blade
How cold steel is, and keen with hunger of blood;
Blue with all malice, like a madman's flash;
And thinly drawn with famishing for flesh.

The weapons are hungry for his blood, "long to nuzzle in the hearts of lads". (One wonders if he remembered that picture of himself as a child, shouldering a toy rifle). It is an unnatural coupling, for the third verse says that the boy's teeth should be "laughing round an apple". While Yeats and others suggest in their poetry that bloodshed might have a positive effect, long-term, Owen is clearly saying do not shed blood, let the young live. 'The Next War', written in hospital, is not one of his better poems but ends with a very definite statement of his beliefs:

> We laughed, — knowing that better men would come,
> And greater wars: when every fighter brags
> He fights on Death, for lives; not men, for flags.

"Flags" reduces patriotism to something petty. He now felt that mankind was artificially split into nations, that no flag was worth killing for and that the only war worth fighting was against disease or other forces that threatened life. On the other hand Yeats was himself a patriot, though not a jingo, and believed that the individual life was not that important. His late poem 'Lapis Lazuli' derides the idea that poets should warn and maintains that the best men are "gay" (in the traditional sense of the word) when faced with tragedy. Man, he seems to have thought, was at his best in combat; one of his favourite symbols was the legendary hero Cuchulain fighting the sea, not because he hoped to win, just because it was there. This made him profoundly unsympathetic to Owen's values and explains the sour comment, "there is every excuse for him, but none for those who like him". Owen, as he knew, had won the M.C., but that did not mean his message needs to be taken seriously.

'War is not murder, war is sacrifice'

Long before 1914, there was a powerful campaign, organised by the National Service League, for universal conscription. It was argued that continental nations, which made all their young men do a stint in the army, were much better prepared than Britain for the war which must eventually come. In peacetime, this campaign made no progress. Throughout most of the nineteenth century it was felt that a man only volunteered to be a soldier if he was no good for anything else, a feeling especially strong in the puritan middle class into which Wilfred Owen was born. (That is the feeling behind the letter of 28 August 1914 which suggests that British Tommies will be no great loss to the world). There was also the argument that they should not be trained to kill people. This was dealt with in a pamphlet written for the League by a clergyman:

> War is not murder, as some fancy, war is sacrifice. The fighting and killing are not of the essence of it, but are the accidents, though the inseparable accidents; and even these, in the wide modern fields where a soldier rarely in his own sight sheds any blood but his own, where he lies on the battle sward not to inflict death but to endure it — even these are mainly purged of savagery and transfigured into devotion. War is not murder, but sacrifice; which is the essence of Christianity. (Quoted David Boulton, *Objection Overruled* [1967], 67).

Owen students will immediately be reminded of 'Exposure', where the soldiers lie on the poetically-named "battle sward" being frozen and shot at, but not killing. Indeed that poem appears to argue that they are Christ-figures offering their lives for others:

> Since we believe not otherwise can kind fires burn;
> Nor ever sun smile true on child, or field, or fruit....
> Therefore, not loath, we lie out here; therefore were born,
> For love of God seems dying.

During the Great War it became normal to compare British soldiers with Christ and the quote "Greater love hath no man than this, that a man lay down his life for his friends" was heard everywhere. "The Church", as one minister recalled, "...had become an instrument of the State, and in too many pulpits the preacher had assumed the role of a recruiting sergeant. Almost every place of worship throughout the length and breadth of the land displayed the Union Jack, generally placed above the Holy Table" (quoted *The Deluge*, 321). The Archbishop of Canterbury supported the Conscription Act, asking only that it should not be applied to clergymen. Since great numbers of people at that time (including Wilfred) came from strongly Christian homes, all this had its effect. After the war religion went into decline but, seventy years on, it is still quite common for us to idealise the soldier. In the popular press, every man who has been in a war, whether he distinguished himself or not, is a 'hero'. We talk about them making the supreme sacrifice, risking their lives for others, their youth, their suffering.

Sentimentalists, like the cleric quoted above, draw a decent veil over the obvious fact that a soldier's job is to kill. This was illustrated by people's reaction to the TV film *Tumbledown*, written by Charles Wood and screened in 1987. The hero, Robert, is an officer who has been badly maimed in the Falklands war and whose experiences are shown in flashbacks. We sympathise with him, because he has been wounded and because he seems a pleasant young man, almost to the end of the film; then there is a short, shocking scene where he is shown bayonetting an Argentinian. Many viewers were deeply repelled and upset. Patriots said the film ought not to have been shown. Presumably the scene was held back because it would have destroyed our sympathy; there is also an implication that Robert cannot bear to remember or speak of it for a very long time.

Bayonet practice is described by Graves in a comic passage which is worth comparing with the pious sentiments of the pamphlet, above:

> The men had to make horrible grimaces and utter blood-curdling yells as they charged. The instructors' faces were set in a permanent ghastly grin. 'Hurt him, now! In at the belly! Tear his guts out!' they would scream, as the men charged the dummies. 'Now that upper swing at his privates with the butt. Ruin his chances for life! No more little Fritzes! ....Naaoh! Anyone would think that you *loved* the bloody swine, patting and stroking 'em like that! BITE HIM, I SAY! STICK YOUR TEETH IN HIM AND WORRY HIM! EAT HIS HEART OUT!' (*Goodbye to All That*, Chapter 21)

This was often "the point at which decent-minded citizens came to regret that they had joined the Army" (M.R.D. Foot, *Art and War* [1990], 56). Reginald Pound described it as "the ghastly exercise in which they were expected to show a fiend's delight" (*The Lost Generation*, 111). I have deliberately quoted two writers who were not against the war in principle. It was disturbing because the bayonet, unlike guns and bombs, involves killing a human being at close quarters. It is the weapon of the speaker in 'Strange Meeting', who "jabbed and killed" his enemy; this emphasises the close connection between them and his personal responsibility. Cynics say we would all be willing to eliminate an unknown Chinaman for a vast sum of money, provided we had to do nothing but press a button. The bayonet is at the opposite end of the scale.

Even using guns and bombs, a sensitive man might still feel guilty. The airman poet Paul Bewsher wrote about "bearing poison" when he bombed towns behind the lines:

> Death, Grief and Pain
> Are what I give.
> O that the slain
> Might live — might live!
> I know them not, for I have blindly killed,
> And nameless hearts with nameless sorrow filled.
> ('Nox Mortis').

Ivor Gurney, the musician who dreamed of Gloucestershire water meadows when on the Somme, and who went mad after the war, also had serious problems with guilt:

> I shot him, and it had to be
> One of us! 'Twas him or me.
> 'Couldn't be helped', and none can blame
> Me, for you would do the same.
>
> My mother, she can't sleep for fear
> Of what might be a-happening here
> To me. Perhaps it might be best
> To die, and set her fears at rest.
>
> For worst is worst, and worry's done.
> Perhaps he was the only son ...
> Yet God keeps still, and does not say
> A word of guidance any way.

Well, if they get me, first I'll find
That boy, and tell him all my mind,
And see who felt the bullet worst,
And ask his pardon, if I durst.

All's a tangle. Here's my job.
A man might rave, or shout, or sob;
And God He takes no sort of heed.
This is a bloody mess indeed.
                                ('The Target').

In France, religious symbols were everywhere, from wayside
shrines and crosses to the famous horizontal Virgin of Albert, who
had been so badly damaged that she seemed about to drop her
baby off the cathedral. Both Gurney, the former cathedral choir-
boy, and Owen, who developed the idea of a meeting after death
in a greater poem, had trouble reconciling this simple religion with
war. Some have called Wilfred a Christian; ex-Christian would be
more accurate. He had been brought up by an intensely religious
mother, had detached himself from the Church in 1913 and
afterwards showed little respect for clerics. He attended services
from time to time, but after leaving Dunsden he did not profess
any religious commitment and made it clear that poetry and the
war were his main interests. Yet he remained deeply attracted to
the teaching of Christ and, like other people, noted that it was
inconsistent with the Church's behaviour. In a long and important
letter, written after his nervous breakdown, he noted that his mind
was running on biblical texts and said this showed that they were
part of his "being":

> I am more and more Christian as I walk the unchristian
> ways of Christendom. Already I have comprehended a light
> which never will filter into the dogma of any national
> church: namely that one of Christ's essential commands
> was: Passivity at any price! Suffer dishonour and disgrace;
> but never resort to arms. Be bullied, be outraged, be killed;
> but do not kill. It may be a chimerical and an ignominious
> principle, but there it is. It can only be ignored: and I think
> pulpit professionals are ignoring it very skilfully and suc-
> cessfully indeed.

He went on to comment that two well-known preachers, whom he had heard in his Dunsden days, were cutting "ridiculous figures" by trying to stay out of the army on account of their "invaluable work". If they had refused on moral grounds he would have admired them. He now described himself as "a conscientious objector with a very seared conscience":

> Christ is literally in no man's land. There men often hear
> His voice: Greater love hath no man than this, that a man
> lay down his life — for a friend.
> Is it spoken in English only and French?
> I do not believe so.
> Thus you see how pure Christianity will not fit in with
> pure patriotism. (Letter 512).

If Christianity was true, it had to be equally true for all nations and could not be mixed up with a patriotic war. He continued to feel anger against "religious men that say it is good to be in that Hell" (Letter 539). A number of short poems on religious issues continue the argument; 'Le Christianisme' notes how statues are battered by shells and has the Catholic saints packed away in cellars, "well out of hearing of our trouble". In 'Soldier's Dream', Jesus fouls up the guns to stop the war but God is "vexed", and sends the warrior angel, Michael, to mend them. Here he is blaspheming mildly but still revealing the influence of his background. Jesus represents love and compassion while his father, the "Field-Marshal God" of 'Inspection', is an authority figure, mindless, loveless. Fathers and sons reappear in a schematic poem, 'The Parable of the Old Man and the Young':

> So Abram rose, and clave the wood, and went,
> And took the fire with him, and a knife.
> And as they sojourned both of them together,
> Isaac the first-born spake and said, My Father,
> Behold the preparations, fire and iron,
> But where the lamb, for this burnt-offering?
> Then Abram bound the youth with belt and straps,
> And builded parapets and trenches there,
> And stretchèd forth the knife to slay his son.
> When lo! an Angel called him out of heaven,
> Saying, Lay not thy hand upon the lad,

Neither do anything to him, thy son.
Behold! Caught in a thicket by its horns,
A Ram. Offer the Ram of Pride instead.

But the old man would not so, but slew his son,
And half the seed of Europe, one by one.

The story of Abraham and Isaac had been taught in Sunday school for generations, and all the little Owens knew it very well. Children of our irreligious age may need to be told that Abraham is a patriarch, father of the Jewish race, and Isaac his only legitimate son, born late in life, whom he loves. God commands him to offer the boy as a sacrifice and Abraham agrees (his mother is not consulted); only when he is raising his knife for the kill does the angel stop him:

> Lay not thine hand upon the lad, neither do thou any thing unto him: for now I know that thou fearest God, seeing thou hast not withheld thy son, thine only son from me. (Genesis 22, 12).

The point of the parable is that God must be obeyed at any cost; once Abraham has proved he is willing to do so there is a happy ending and he is allowed to sacrifice a ram instead. In the first twelve lines Owen sticks quite closely to the language of the Authorised Version, though introducing parapets and trenches to show he is talking about the war. But he substitutes a shockingly different ending. The old man is free to sacrifice "the ram of pride instead" but, out of pure perversity, he kills his son. As in 'Inspection' a young, innocent victim, representative of countless others, is sacrificed to a capricious authority.

According to the creed in which Owen had been raised, God had also sacrificed his son, Jesus. Now a generation of young men was being killed off while their parents watched in anguish but did not try to stop the war. There is no need to bring in Wilfred's strained relationship with Tom Owen since it is obvious that the war was being fought by young men, directed by men above military age. The ruling class lost an unduly high proportion of its sons, since junior officers ran special risks, and this must surely have convinced them and others that they were ready to make any sacrifice.

When Asquith's eldest son was killed in 1916 "the death of the Prime Minister's son in action at last convinced the French that we were with them to the very end" (*The Lost Generation*, 269). It could be called the extreme of callousness or supreme unselfishness, depending on your point of view. Owen, Sassoon, Graves and Sitwell were all hostile to the old men.

Jesus was different, since every wayside cross emphasised that he was a fellow-victim. Owen's poem 'At a Calvary near the Ancre' shows that he still looked on him with some reverence:

> One ever hangs where shelled roads part.
> In this war He too lost a limb,
> But His disciples hide apart;
> And now the Soldiers bear with Him.
>
> Near Golgotha strolls many a priest,
> And in their faces there is pride
> That they were flesh-marked by the Beast
> By whom the gentle Christ's denied.
>
> The scribes on all the people shove
> And bawl allegiance to the state,
> But they who love the greater love
> Lay down their life, they do not hate.

The message of these poems, taken together, would seem to be that the Church is thoroughly corrupt. The *national* church, as Owen's letter stressed, since the Pope had tried to stop the war and some Christians had gone to prison rather than take part. But once the Church got involved with the State, it was finished morally. God is a remote patriarch, who quite possibly wants the war to continue; only Christ is with the soldiers, sharing their agony (bearing the cross). But, as we have already seen, a soldier cannot truly be described as Christ-like. Much of his life might be spent being bombarded in the trenches and enduring other agonies, but, when all is said, he was there to kill.

Owen was fully conscious of this and hinted in 'Spring Offensive' that they had damned themselves by choosing to "enter hell". Some poems, notably 'Inspection', show guilt about his role as an officer, and he wrote to Osbert Sitwell that his job involved "teaching Christ to lift his cross by numbers, and how to adjust his crown; and not to imagine he thirst till after the last halt" (Letter 634). Finally, in 'Strange Meeting', he places himself in hell because he has killed his friend — not "laid down his life for a friend", but died fighting.

So, in the end, he has an ambivalent view of soldiers. They suffered, far more than those who were not in uniform, and it was tempting to compare them with Christ, but this was too simple. He tried, not very successfully, to resolve the contradictions in 'Apologia pro Poemate meo', which was written after an appeal from Graves to "write more optimistically ... a poet should have a spirit above wars" (C.L. 596). Owen replied, in effect, that life at the front had its compensations but he was not going to comfort those at home by pretending it was all clean fun:

> I, too, saw God through mud, —
> The mud that cracked on cheeks when wretches smiled.
> War brought more glory to their eyes than blood,
> And gave their laughs more glee than shakes a child.
>
> Merry it was to laugh there —
> Where death becomes absurd and life absurder.
> For power was on us as we slashed bones bare
> Not to feel sickness or remorse of murder.

He has found friendship in the ranks, he says:

> I have made fellowships —
> Untold of happy lovers in old song ...

— the bond which ties these men together is stronger than any between lovers. After some more verses which I will not inflict on the reader, the poem ends:

> I have perceived much beauty
> In the hoarse oaths that kept our courage straight;
> Heard music in the silentness of duty;
> Found peace where shell-storms spouted reddest spate.
> Nevertheless, except you share
> With them in hell the sorrowful dark of hell,

Whose world is but the trembling of a flare
And heaven but as the highway for a shell,

You shall not hear their mirth:
You shall not come to think them well content
By any jest of mine. These men are worth
Your tears. You are not worth their merriment.

Who is "you"? Does he mean those in high places who callously keep men at the front, or everyone who has not been there? From the words "except you share" it would seem that the latter is meant. Men at war are "wretches", they curse and are "foul", and he does not shrink from describing what they do as "murder". Yet there is a positive side, most of all in the friendship which springs up between them. Richard Aldington said, in the prologue to *Death of a Hero*, that this was "just a human relation, a comradeship, an undemonstrative exchange of sympathies between ordinary men racked to extremity under a great common strain in a great common danger". (He added that such friendships were platonic, and that few survived the Armistice). Graves' poem 'Two Fusiliers' is about just such a friendship, and states convincingly that men who have been through the war together will always have much in common. But 'Apologia', written in response to Graves, goes further, and appears to suggest that soldiers have shared a high and holy experience which makes them permanently superior to the rest of the human race.

It is a poor poem ("beauty/ duty", indeed!), but it is interesting to note how those who had survived the war singled out 'Apologia' — and 'Greater Love', which is almost as bad — for special praise. The feeling persisted that they had made a far greater sacrifice than anyone could understand and, therefore, could never be honoured enough. Owen clearly did not believe that war in itself was honourable, but his weaker poems do show a slight feeling of contempt for those who had not been there.

Any man who risks his life has to be respected. Yet the soldier has always been an ambivalent figure, especially as he runs little risk in modern high-tech wars. In January 1993, for instance, President George Bush ordered a bombing raid on Iraq and, when his planes came back safely, spoke emotionally about their "young crews who did God's work". Among the victims of that raid was a young woman, Amira Uydaeel, who had been doing the unheroic job of a hotel receptionist. She got the guests inside the shelter, came out to see if anyone was left, and was killed. Who was braver, the uniformed man firing missiles from a great distance or the unarmed woman trying to save lives? From 'The Next War', we may guess what Owen would have thought, and he might also have made barbed remarks about Bush's reference to God.

It could be asked why we constantly praise soldiers, call them heroes, send them knitted socks and Christmas puddings etc., when we show none of this concern for, say, firefighters and lifeboatmen, who risk their lives for others without killing. The answer, as Owen knew, has to do with reasons of state.

Fat Civilians

"A Senior Lieutenant has turned up from Leave", Wilfred wrote home in October 1918, "...He has returned from his first visit to London utterly disgusted with England's indifference to the real meaning of the war as we understand it" (Letter 667). Men were constantly going back and forth between England and the trenches and finding that the contrast, as we would now say, blew their minds. In France it must have seemed even more glaring; Barbusse has men visiting Paris on leave and feeling they are in a foreign country. At first they are overwhelmed because everything is so splendid, then they see a "ridiculous tableau" about the war which upsets them, but do not have the courage to criticise it. After that a patriotic lady gushes over them:

> "How superb a charge must be, eh? All those masses of men advancing like they do in a holiday procession, and the trumpets playing a rousing air in the fields! And the dear little soldiers that can't be held back and shouting 'Vive la France!' and even laughing as they die!" (Under Fire, chapter 22).

Sassoon was the first English writer to attack such people; elderly men clucking over the casualty lists, cheering crowds, women in music halls singing vulgar patriotic songs. This feeling was not confined to men; Vera Brittain, returning from nursing in France, was astounded that her parents could only talk about food rationing and the shortage of servants. A fine example is 'Recruiting', by E.A. Mackintosh (killed 1917). He was not a great poet, but his work does give an exceptionally clear and pure voice to certain basic feelings (his 'In Memoriam' is perhaps the most distressing poem of the war). During sick leave in 1916-17, his feelings seem to have changed:

> 'Lads, you're wanted, go and help',
> On the railway carriage wall
> Stuck the poster, and I thought
> Of the hands that penned the call.
>
> Fat civilians wishing they
> 'Could go out and fight the Hun'.
> Can't you see them thanking God
> That they're over forty-one?
>
> Girls with feathers, vulgar songs —
> Washy verse on England's need —
> God — and don't we damned well know
> How the message ought to read.
>
> 'Lads, you're wanted! over there',
> Shiver in the morning dew,
> More poor devils like yourselves
> Waiting to be killed by you.
>
> Go and help to swell the names
> In the casualty lists.
> Help to make a column's stuff
> For the blasted journalists.
>
> Help to keep them nice and safe
> From the wicked German foe.
> Don't let him come over here!
> 'Lads, you're wanted — out you go'.

By the halfway point of the war, the Germans have become fellow-victims while the folks at home are the real enemy. Mackintosh concludes his poem by urging the young men to go to

France, not because the old men tell them to but because it is better to "live clean or go out quick" than resemble the old men in any way. "Come and die", the poem ends. Presumably this is why he went back, like Sassoon and Owen. "England one by one had fled to France", Owen wrote ('Smile, Smile, Smile'), and the same note is struck on the last page of Williamson's *Patriot's Progress*. When the hero, John Bullock, comes home minus a leg and an older man tells him that England is grateful, he replies, "We are England". Civilians will never understand.

Death of a Hero (1929), by Richard Aldington, is the book which expresses this disgust most profoundly. Aldington (1892-1962) was married to the Imagist poet 'H.D.' and had moved in advanced literary circles before the war. His novel, whose name is not intended to be taken seriously, is an attack on patriotism, religion, bad art and just about everything else the bourgeoisie held sacred, attitudes which he believed had made the war possible. Some of the attacks are so shrill, some characters so improbable that we are tempted to call it a bitter and unbalanced book. (For instance, the hero's mother is entertaining a lover half her age when she gets the telegram, and even his death does not long put her off. Other women in the novel behave no better).

However, the last part, set during the war, is superb. The 'hero', George Winterbourne, is killed, like Owen, in the early hours of 4 November 1918 (this is no accident, and shows the respect he had won from the avant-garde). In fact he has committed suicide by standing up in the face of enemy fire. Like everyone else, George has had a bad time in the trenches, but what really breaks his spirit is going on leave. His wife is having an affair, London is full of prostitutes, and smart people are carrying on inane conversations as normal. "He felt very uncomfortable, like a death's-head at a feast" (3, 12). A character based on the non-combatant T.S. Eliot absurdly asks him if he spends his leisure reading and painting. But any talent he possessed before the war seems to have been lost, and when he dies there is no one to mourn him.

For those who survived, there was the added pain of knowing that younger people were not interested. Aldington ended his novel with a poem lamenting the dead and noting the apathy of the new generation:

'Why should they bore us for ever
With an old quarrel and the names of dead men
We never knew, and dull forgotten battles?'

Vera Brittain had a traumatic encounter with Oxford women a few years younger than herself, who had not been bereaved. More recently, Richard Adams, a Second World War veteran, has dramatised the gulf between those who have been there and those who haven't in *Watership Down* (1972). This remarkable novel is only superficially a children's adventure story. In reality, it is about survival, about a little group of rabbits (men) coming through tremendous dangers together, about a democracy (England) taking on a totalitarian state and winning. It is not in any way pro-war but feels that "nearly always there are those who want to fight and those who do not but feel they cannot avoid it" (Chapter 46). One of the stories it tells is of two rabbits who endure unimaginable suffering to save their tribe. When they come back, still conscious of the horror, they are met with blank indifference:

> 'Here, do me a favour, old fellow, will you?' said the buck. 'That fighting — I wasn't born when it finished'.
> 'But surely you know the Owsla captains who were?' said Rabscuttle.
> 'I wouldn't be seen dead with them', said the buck.
>
> 'What, that white-whiskered old bunch? What do we want to know about them?'
> 'What they did', said Rabscuttle.
> 'That war lark, old fellow?' said the first buck.
>
> 'That's all finished now. That's got nothing to do with us'....
> 'It was all a very wicked thing', said another doe.
>
> 'Shameful, really. If nobody fought in wars there wouldn't be any, would there? But you can't get old rabbits to see that'. (Chapter 31).

There is a generational conflict here, and also a conflict between the sexes, since the does (female rabbits, who do not play a great part in *Watership Down*) are making a traditional female argument against war which deserves to be taken more seriously. But the pain expressed by those who feel that their sacrifices were not valued is real. So is the danger that future generations will not learn from the past.

Owen shares some of this bitterness against civilians. The man in 'The Dead-Beat' has been demoralised by "Blighty", and in 'S.I.W.', when the soldier at the end of his tether commits suicide, it is his family who are blamed:

> Patting goodbye, doubtless they told the lad
> He'd always show the Hun a brave man's face;
> Father would sooner him dead than in disgrace, —
> Was proud to see him going, aye, and glad.
> Perhaps his mother whimpered how she'd fret
> Until he got a nice safe wound to nurse.
> Sisters would wish girls too could shoot, charge, curse ...
> Brothers — would send his favourite cigarette.

Even at the end they have to be protected from knowing that he died by his own hand. But, in 'The Next War' and 'Arms and the Boy', Owen makes it clear that he does not want the next generation to go through the same thing.

1914-18 was the last war in which civilians could remain insulated from the truth while great numbers of their husbands, brothers and sons were dying. As a matter of fact, some thirty million civilians died in Europe (compared to about nine million soldiers) of starvation, influenza and other diseases let loose by the war. It is also true that in the South African war, at the turn of the century, Kitchener had herded women and children into the concentration camps which he invented, and thousands had died. But that was not how it looked from Britain. There were some Zeppelin raids on London or the east coast, in which some civilians died, but, comparatively speaking, they lived in comfort and safety. That made the attitude of those who wanted a "fight to the finish" all the more unbearable. If we are to believe Sassoon, Aldington, Graves and others there was scarcely a decent person left at home:

> Winterbourne heard them constantly using the phrase
> 'three hundred thousand men', as if they were cows or

pence or radishes.... He wanted to seize the people in the room, the people in authority, everyone not directly in the War, and shout to them: '...You must stop it, you've got to stop it!' (*Death of a Hero*, 3, 12).

Yet, of course, life is not quite so simple. As soldiers, Owen and Sassoon were in a strong position to denounce the war, but there were other soldiers who believed just as strongly that it should go on until Germany was smashed. Among civilians, attitudes ranged from Bottomley to the small minority of pacifists, the difference being that jingoes spoke their minds loudly while those who hated the war were often afraid to say so. It was a civilian, Helen Hamilton, who wrote one of the better wartime poems about just the sort of attitudes that enraged Sassoon:

THE GHOULS

You strange old ghouls,
Who gloat with dulled old eyes,
Over those lists,
Those dreadful lists,
To see what name
Of friend, relation,
However distant,
May be appended
To your private Roll of Honour.
Unknowingly you draw, it seems,
From their young bodies,
Dead young bodies,
Fresh life,
New value,
Now that yours are ebbing.
You strange old ghouls,
Who gloat with dulled old eyes,
Over those lists,
Those dreadful lists,
Of young men dead.

(It is, perhaps, relevant that Leslie Gunston wrote his 'Hymn of Love to England' in stirring Victorian metres while those who questioned the received attitudes often did so in the rhythm of the future, free verse.)

In the next generation, technology would break down the distinction between fighting men and everyone else. There was outrage when Hitler's planes bombed the open city of Guernica in 1937, but both sides would do worse things in 1939-45. In that war, one in eight British casualties was a civilian and worldwide there were far more civilians than soldiers killed. Bombing from the air is the key to this. Those who send the bombers always say that they do not intend to kill civilians, but in practice this always happens, and if you add the effects of radiation (Hiroshima) or the destruction of water and sewage systems (Iraq) the damage to the old, the weak and the unborn spreads. Most countries have their memorial to the unknown soldier, but nothing for the unknown civilian or child.

We need not ask what Wilfred would have thought about the deaths of non-combatants for, as it happens, we know. In a letter written the week before he was killed, he said:

> Did I tell you that five healthy girls died of fright in one night at the last village. The people in England and France who thwarted a peaceable retirement of the enemy from these areas are therefore now sacrificing aged French peasants and charming French children to our guns. Shells made by women in Birmingham are at this moment burying little children alive not very far from here. (Letter 672).

It is almost as if he was prophesying the shape of wars to come.

Glory of Women

"And the women? Oh, don't let's talk about the women", wrote Aldington with heavy irony in *Death of a Hero*. "They were splendid, wonderful. Such devotion, such devotion! How they comforted the troops! Oh, wonderful, beyond all praise! They got the vote for it, you know.... Whatever should we have done without them? White feathers, and all that, you know. Oh, the women were marvellous" (2, 6).

Almost as soon as the decision to go to war had been taken, every effort was made to get women involved. Posters exhorted young men "Women of Britain say Go", or asked "Have you any women folk worth defending?". "We don't want to lose you but we think you ought to go", ran the famous music-hall song by Phyllis Dare. (At least two poets called the girls who sang recruiting songs "harlots"). Later when the flow of men slowed down there were attempts to shame them; one poster had a woman asking, "Will you go or must I?"

Mrs Pankhurst and her daughter Christabel, who had been waging all-out but non-violent war on the government up to August 1914, immediately turned round and became more patriotic than anyone. (Her younger daughter Sylvia was always against the war; Mrs Fawcett's National Union of Women's Suffrage Societies opposed it up to the last moment, but then swung into line). It can now be seen that this was a brilliant tactical move. Not only did it win the vote for them in 1918; it also got thousands of upper and middle-class women out of the home and gave them the chance to prove that they could work as well as anyone, and not just at traditional tasks like nursing. Photographs of smiling girls driving buses, working on the land and wearing a variety of uniforms suggest that they thoroughly enjoyed their new experiences. Society soon grew used to them doing these jobs; less easy, for some, was the sight of women making shells:

> Their hands should minister unto the flame of life,
> Their fingers guide
> The rosy teat, swelling with milk,
> To the eager mouth of the suckling babe ....
> But now....
> They must take part in defacing and destroying the
>   natural body.
> (Mary Gabrielle Collins, 'Women at Munition Making').

After the war, there was a certain feeling that women had done quite well out of it. There was also the obvious fact that British women were in little personal danger, and very few ever saw the front at first hand. For this reason, as Vera Brittain said, there was a "terrible barrier of knowledge by which War cut off the men who possessed it from the women" (*Testament of Youth*, 215). They might say, like the girl in 'S.I.W', that they wished they could "go", but both knew this meant nothing. Men were constantly told that they

149

had to save "women and children" from unspeakable horrors, and poor, outraged Belgium was drawn on recruiting posters as a woman crying out to be avenged. England was also portrayed as a woman:

> Sons of mine, I hear you thrilling
> To the trumpet call of war;
> Gird ye then, I give you freely
> As I gave your sires before,
> All the noblest of the children I in love and anguish bore.
> (W.N. Hodgson, 'England to her Sons').

Binyon's 'For the Fallen', which opens

> With proud thanksgiving, a mother for her children,
> England mourns for her dead across the sea

uses the same image. Not a mother protecting her children, as you might expect, but one like the white-haired woman in the poster who says "Go! it's your duty, lad". She is treated more sourly by Owen in one of his minor poems, 'The Kind Ghosts', about a woman who appears to be Britannia, and who is unaware of the sacrifices of young men:

> She sleeps on soft, last breaths; but no ghost looms
> Out of the stillness of her palace wall,
> Her wall of boys on boys and dooms on dooms.
>
> She dreams of golden gardens and sweet glooms,
> Not marvelling why her roses never fall
> Nor what red mouths were torn to make their blooms.
>
> The shades keep down which well might roam her hall.
> Quiet their blood lies in her crimson rooms
> And she is not afraid of their footfall.
>
> They move not from her tapestries, their pall,
> Nor pace her terraces, their hecatombs,
> Lest aught she be disturbed, or grieved at all.

This female figure is asleep, having beautiful dreams, while everyone is too polite to tell her what is happening. In this climate, some men inevitably felt bitter, and the actions of some women did not help. Robert Graves quotes a "typical document of this time", a letter from a woman calling herself "a Little Mother":

> ...we women, who demand to be heard, will tolerate no such cry as 'Peace! Peace!' where there is no peace.... There is only one temperature for the women of the British race, and that is white heat.... We women pass on the human ammunition of 'only sons' to fill up the gaps, so that when the 'common soldier' looks back before going 'over the top' he may see the women of the British race at his heels, reliable, dependent, uncomplaining.... Women are created for the purpose of giving life, and men to take it. (*Goodbye to All That*, Chapter 21).

Women who gave white feathers to men not in khaki were possibly quite a small number; a survey in the 1950s found only one still alive who admitted having done it. But (like the men shot at dawn) they became a symbol of everything that was wrong with the war. It is my impression that they were not popular, even then, not only because they often picked on the wrong men but also because their conduct was felt to be deeply unnatural:

> You shame us women.
> Can't you see it isn't decent,
> To flout and goad men into doing
> What is not asked of you?
> (Helen Hamilton, 'The Jingo-Woman').

There were others who went to the opposite extreme. Sylvia Pankhurst's *Dreadnought* published Sassoon's statement; the No Conscription Fellowship was kept going by women who took over when the men were arrested, and women from all over Europe attended a peace congress at The Hague in 1915. There was even a suggestion that a thousand volunteers should get between the armies to stop them, but this failed because not enough women came forward. Perhaps it should have been tried. But the great majority, lacking votes, power and in most cases higher education, believed what they were told and tried to help the war effort. They had not started it; they suffered constant fear and agonising bereavement, but some poets still attacked them:

> You love us when we're heroes, home on leave,
> Or wounded in a mentionable place

Sassoon wrote in 'Glory of Women'. "Mentionable" implies that they are too sheltered to be told the worst details, and they are also blamed for listening "with delight" to tales of "dirt and danger". In 'Their Frailty' he accuses them, more convincingly, of ignoring broad issues and only being concerned with their personal lives:

> Husbands and sons and lovers; everywhere
> They die; War bleeds us white
> Mothers and wives and sweethearts, — they don't care
> So long as He's all right.

"I think they love war, for all their lamenting over the sons and lovers", Sassoon wrote in his diary for 20 January 1917. "All the dying and wounds and mud and bloodiness — at a safe distance — gave them a great kick, and excited them to an almost unbearable pitch of amorousness", wrote Aldington in the prologue to *Death of a Hero*. More gently, the war-damaged Ivor Gurney lamented:

> And for my Country, God knows my heart, and men to
>   me
> Were dear there; I was friend also of every look of sun or
>   rain;
> It has betrayed as evil women wantonly a man their toy.
>   ('There is Nothing')

and there is the same feeling in Pound's image of the "old bitch gone in the teeth", England.

Where does Owen fit in? Since he was one of several men who expressed deep bitterness about the war, some critics have gone a step further and claimed that he disliked women, which is untrue. "It is noticeable that, in his war poetry, Owen had no pity to spare for the suffering of bereaved women", writes C. Day Lewis in his introduction to the 1963 edition. As a human being, he was well aware of it, writing to a friend of Susan's whose son had been killed, "I have endured unnameable tortures in France; but I know that I have not suffered by this war as you have and are suffering" (Letter 530). He also knew exactly how his mother would react to his death, and his letters from his second tour in France invariably try to reassure her.

The 'anti-women' allegation rests on two planks; the fact that he never had a serious relationship with one and the remark, "All women, without exception, *annoy* me' (Letter 238), which is no more than most of us have said at some time about the opposite sex. He also complained to Mary (Letter 259) that "it is quite impossible to talk soberly and intellectually" with French girls. There is no doubt that he had deep sexual inhibitions and we cannot know how he would have dealt with them if he had lived. But his attitude to women was friendly and egalitarian. In his dealings with his mother and Mary, whom he thought of all the time on the freezing battlefield, or Henriette, "that young and ardent nature" (Letter 250), or Madame Leger and her daughter, or the Edinburgh ladies who took him slum-visiting, or Marie Dauthieu for whom he wrote some romantic verses, there is no trace of negative feelings. Mary Newboult, who was fourteen when she met him, recalled:

> In those days I was a very shy and inarticulate girl but I do remember how very easy Wilfred was to talk to. He had the gift of drawing people out of themselves.... I remember too how he helped me with my homework.... It was just wonderful for me to find someone like Wilfred to be interested in a raw, awkward schoolgirl such as I was. (C.L.,594).

He was also willing — and this was quite unusual — to take women seriously on an intellectual level. Mrs Browning, as I argued, was a major influence; he revered her together with Keats and named her (Letter 538) as another reason for not falling in love. Among living poets, he admired Olwen Joergens, Margaret Sackville, and, presumably, Edith Sitwell and her colleagues in *Wheels*. The question of whether their talent was equal to men's, often discussed today, seems not even to have occurred to him.

His war poems do show a feeling that all civilians (see above) were blind to what was going on. There are the women who garland soldiers in 'The Send-Off', the girls who look away from the wounded man in 'Disabled', and the faithless wife and silly sister in 'The Dead-Beat' and 'S.I.W'. In the last two poems, though, the women are only part of a group of civilians which is dominated by aggressive older men. It would seem to be the patriarchs whom Owen really dislikes, judging by his poems on religious themes, and 'Smile, Smile, Smile'. Any resentment he may feel against women is extremely mild compared to the searing attacks from Aldington and Sassoon. We should also note the "pallor of girls' brows" in 'Anthem for Doomed Youth' and the couplet which sees women as a source of comfort:

> For girls' breasts are the clear white Acropole,
> Where our own mothers' tears shall heal us whole.
> ('A New Heaven').

There remains 'Greater Love', that overrated poem which was originally titled, 'To any Beautiful Woman':

> Red lips are not so red
> As the stained stones kissed by the English dead.
> Kindness of wooed and wooer
> Seems shame to their love pure.
> O Love, your eyes lose lure
> When I behold eyes blinded in my stead!
>
> Your slender attitude
> Trembles not exquisite like limbs knife-skewed,
> Rolling and rolling there
> Where God seems not to care;
> Till the fierce love they bear
> Cramps them in death's extreme decrepitude.
>
> Your voice sings not so soft, —
> Though even as wind murmuring through raftered loft,—
> Your dear voice is not dear,
> Gentle, and evening clear,
> As theirs whom none now hear,
> Now earth has stopped their piteous mouths that
>   coughed.

> Heart, you were never hot
> Nor large, nor full like hearts made great with shot;
> And though your hand be pale,
> Paler are all which trail
> Your cross through flame and hail:
> Weep, you may weep, for you may touch them not.

This poem will always have its admirers, but Owen himself listed it under "doubtful", when planning his book, and might not in the end have passed it for publication. The popularity stems from the fact that it raises soldiers to a pinnacle of suffering and sacrifice, trailing "*your* cross through fire and hail" (my italics) so that the non-combatant reader feels guilty. Apart from the reference to God not caring, it could quite easily be read as pro-war. It is only the English dead who are pitied, and the emphasis on their agony is not as subversive as it may seem. By that stage, the public had surely stopped thinking that men at the front were having a jolly time, but propagandists then and since have often used the suffering as a perverse argument for going on with the war. If men have died for a great cause, for their country, and so on, who are we to question it? We can only acknowledge our inferiority, and weep.

That is part of what is wrong with the poem. There is also the late-Romantic imagery of red lips and pale hands (he had been reading Swinburne) which, as Yeats said, leaves a flavour of sucked sugar-stick. Sassoon recorded that he had had to warn his friend against "over-luscious" writing. And the picture of the dead kissing "stained stones" (mud, surely?) seems much prettier than the real thing, as described in a better poem:

> And thud! flump! thud! down the steep steps came
>   thumping
> And sploshing in the flood, deluging muck,
> The sentry's body
>   ('The Sentry').

One cannot imagine a word like "sploshing" in the elegant and slightly decadent 'Greater Love'.

That does not mean, though, that the poem is anti-women. Paradoxically, it suggests that Wilfred found them attractive but could not indulge himself when he had sterner and more painful matters on his mind. This is a fairly common male attitude (women are for relaxation, war is for real). It also harks back to his teenage poem, 'Deep under turfy grass and heavy clay', in which he contemplated the (female) victims of a disaster and asked himself how anyone could be so callous as to think of love. Brecht would express a similar feeling between the wars:

> What kind of an age is it
> in which to talk of trees is almost a crime
> because it implies an indifference to so many horrors?
> ('To Posterity').

Ultimately, the poem fits into the pattern of Wilfred's life, so far as we know it; his work came first, and he would write occasionally about love, but not get too involved too soon.

There has always been a feeling that war is not women's business, and when it happens they should keep quiet, apart from loyally supporting the men in their small way. During the Gulf war, for instance, a certain right-wing intellectual said that the actress Emma Thompson, who had spoken against it, ought to be knitting for the troops. This attitude is too crude to be voiced officially; instead, every effort is made to show the Army as a modern equal opportunities employer. We no longer hear of "men", but of "servicemen and servicewomen", or "lads and lasses", if you prefer. Women actually took part in the Gulf war, sometimes leaving their children; British viewers were able to see a female American soldier saying no, it wouldn't bother her to kill. I am not convinced that this is progress.

Some of this was foreseen by Olive Schreiner, whose work influenced several young people in the years before 1914. She pointed out that, with increasing technical progress, women would soon be able to take part in any kind of work, including war. But she believed that if they had the choice they would reject it:

> There is, perhaps, no woman ... who could look down upon
> a battlefield covered with slain, but the thought would rise
> in her, 'So many mother's sons! So many bodies brought
> into the world to lie there! So many months of weariness

and pain while bones and muscles were shaped within; so many hours of anguish and struggle that breath might be; so many baby mouths drawing life at women's breasts; — all this, that men might lie with glazed eyeballs, and swollen bodies, and fixed, blue, unclosed mouths, and great limbs tossed — this, that an acre of ground might be manured with human flesh, that next year's grass or poppies or karoo bushes may spring up greener and redder, where they have lain, or that the sand of a plain may have a glint of white bones!' And we cry, 'Without an inexorable cause, this should not be!' (*Woman and Labour* [1911], Chapter 4).

"Was it for this the clay grew tall?".... Olive Schreiner, who had seen the effects of war in her native South Africa, was here making exactly the same point as Owen in 'Futility'. For, of course, women suffered too, though in a less obvious way. Far from finding replacements for the men who died, like the heartless females in Aldington's novel, a whole generation of European women never married. For bereaved mothers, it was possibly even harder — "there was no comfort for the woman whose three sons were killed on the Somme and who stood on the doorstep for ten years calling to her dead boys among the children playing in the gutter" (Jeremy Seabrook, *The Unprivileged* (1967), 63). Their suffering, on the whole, went unrecorded. It should also be obvious that they could not be blamed for the war when they did not even have votes. What is true is that they lacked the confidence to protest in large numbers; even Susan had to be persuaded by her son to find "courage to speak" (Letter 666).

It has been pointed out that Owen revered motherhood, seeing the earth in 'Spring Offensive' as a mother trying to defend her children. He shared the 'female' urge — to protect life, much more than the 'male' urge — to fight. Yet the men in that poem shake off the brambles, "sorrowing arms" which attempt to hold them back. Other poets also seem to have felt that women, with their alternative values, had to be rejected while the war was going on. As Mackintosh wrote to his fiancée in his usual simple and moving style, a month before he was killed:

God knows — my dear — I did not want
To rise and leave you so,

But the dead men's hands were beckoning
And I knew that I must go.
> ('To Sylvia').

Sassoon had the same vision of being summoned by dead men in the poem which he first called 'Death's Brotherhood'. Owen in 1918 also felt this pull, although he was thinking of his responsibility to the living rather than the dead:

For leaning out last midnight on my sill,
I heard the sighs of men, that have no skill
To speak of their distress, no, nor the will!
A voice I know. And this time I must go.
> ('The Calls')

Whether he was right to ignore the appeal from the 'feminine' side of his nature is still open to debate.

Fresher fields than Flanders

Well before Owen's time, there had been war poets. Housman was popular in the years 1914-18, as much of his work is about young men going overseas and dying; so was Thomas Hardy, who had written an important group of poems at the turn of the century about the Boer war. Many people quoted 'The Man he Killed', based on a soldier's reminiscences:

Yes; quaint and curious war is!
You shoot a fellow down
You'd treat if met where any bar is,
Or help to half-a-crown.

He was greatly admired by Sassoon, who would have appreciated the internationalism of 'His Country':

I journeyed from my native spot
Across the south sea shine,
And found that people in hall and cot
Laboured and suffered each his lot
Even as I did mine...
I asked me: 'Whom have I to fight,

And whom have I to dare,
And whom to weaken, crush, and blight?
My country seems to have kept in sight
On my way everywhere'.

Sassoon, in turn, was glad to find that Hardy, who had published some mildly patriotic poems after 1914, nevertheless liked the controversial parts of *The Old Huntsman*. Owen did not at first admire him, preferring the more romantic Yeats, but Sassoon urged him to read *The Dynasts*, and, as noted, it had some influence on 'The Show'. He probably got the word "pity" either from there or from Hardy's 'The Pity of It' (1915), which points out that English and Germans have the same cultural roots. Hardy had also noted, in 'A Christmas Ghost-Story' (1899), that Christian countries generally ignored what Christ had said. So the young war poets were not quite without literary ancestors.

Hardy, of course, had not been to war — had not even been alive in the Napoleonic period — and this raises the question of whether he was qualified to write about it. Owen's biographer, Jon Stallworthy, suggests in his witty 'Poem about Poems about Vietnam' that the answer is no:

The poets of another time —
Owen with a rifle-butt
between his paper and the slime,
Donne quitting Her pillow to cut
a quill — knew that in love and war
dispatches from the front are all.
We believe them, they were there,
when you were at the Albert Hall.

It is a telling point. There were too many bad war poems (and paintings) by people who had not been there, but there were also bad poems by people who had, because experience does not in itself give the power to write well. You could also argue that modern war is not restricted to the battle zone. It reaches into our homes, takes our children, affects the way we speak and the standards of public life. One of the best poems about the South African war ('Drummer Hodge') was written by Hardy, who had never visited the country, and one of the best Vietnam poems, about the adoption of Asian orphans, is by a non-combatant, James Laughlin. It is even possible for a poet to use a battle six centuries ago:

> She sat on a willow-trunk
> watching
> part of the battle of Crecy
> (Miroslav Holub, 'The Fly')

to make a serious point about modern times.

War is universal; that is, it raises fundamental questions of good and evil. Each war generates its own images, some more powerful than others; poppies and barbed wire from 1914-18, the mushroom cloud from Hiroshima, burning oil-wells and limping sea-birds from the Gulf 1991. These images become part of the common stock and go on resonating long after the war is over. So it is not impossible for a person who has not 'been there' to write poetry about some aspect of it. Obviously, though, the best poems are likely to come from someone who has the talent and is in the front line (not necessarily as a combatant); Owen in World War One, Keith Douglas in World War Two.

In the 1930s, younger poets grew up admiring Owen. Stephen Spender's 'Ultima Ratio Regum' has the same theme as 'Futility', transferring the scene from the snowy fields of France to the olive groves of Spain. It was the Spanish war, and the rise of Fascism, which convinced many who had reacted against the ethos of 1914-18 that a second European war could not be avoided. One of them was Herbert Read, who had been embarrassed by being chosen for the Yeats anthology instead of Owen:

> I was an exact contemporary of Wilfred Owen and shared the same experiences in the First World War. His war poetry has meant much to me both as the most exact and profound description of those shared experiences and as a technical development in the art of verse.... Though we fought the same battles, I never met Owen.... But he became my brother, in his passive suffering, in his acceptance of a cruel destiny. (quoted T.J. Walsh, *A Tribute to Wilfred Owen*, 1964).

In 'To a Conscript of 1940' Read pointed out that this war might be necessary but should not be approached in a romantic spirit:

> We think we gave in vain. The world was not renewed.
> There was hope in the homestead and anger in the streets.
> But the old world was restored and we returned
> To the dreary field and workshop, and the immemorial
>   feud
>
> Of rich and poor. Our victory was our defeat....
>
> But you, my brother and my ghost, if you can go
> Knowing that there is no reward, no certain use
> In all your sacrifice, then honour is reprieved.

The generation of 1940 seems to have felt much the same. Sidney Keyes, the youngest poet to be killed, noted in 'Advice for a Journey' that they did not have the "iron certitude which swung our fathers" but took some comfort from the memory of the older war poets:

> Others have come before you. The immortal
> Live like reflections and their frozen faces
> Will give you courage to ignore the subtle
> Sneer of the gentian and the iceworn pebble.

The same note is struck in 'All Day It Has Rained', dedicated to the memory of Edward Thomas, by Alun Lewis (killed 1944). Despite his own strong anti-Fascist commitment, he was careful to distance himself from jingoes, describing how he

> thought of the quiet dead and the loud celebrities
> Exhorting us to slaughter, and the herded refugees.

Some sections of the reading public expected a new wave of poets to appear immediately, getting memorable poems in print while the war was still going on. When this did not happen, there was a cry of 'Where are the War Poets?' This question was partly answered by the brilliant Keith Douglas, writing in 1943, who thought that the best poems would appear afterwards:

> Why are there no poets like Owen and Sassoon who lived

with the fighting troops and wrote of their experiences while they were enduring them?

(This is inexact; Owen wrote his poems behind the lines). Douglas went on:

> ....There are such poets, but they do not write. They do not write because there is nothing new, from a soldier's point of view, about this war except its mobile character....
>
> Hell cannot be let loose twice: it was let loose in the Great War and it is the same old hell now. The hardships, pain and boredom; the behaviour of the living and the appearance of the dead, were so accurately described by the poets of the Great War that every day on the battlefields of the western desert — and no doubt on the Russian battlefields as well — their poems are illustrated. Almost all that a modern poet on active service is inspired to write, would be tautological.... Nor can we produce a body of long range poetry inspired by shocking news items. The poet at home can only make valuable comments on social and political issues. ('Poets in this War', *Times Literary Supplement*, May 1943).

Douglas (killed 1944) was essentially a modernist; Rosenberg was his great inspiration and only one of his major poems seems to have been influenced by Owen:

> Perched on a great fall of air
> a pilot or angel looking down
> on some eccentric chart, a plain
> dotted with useless furniture,
> discerns dying on the sand vehicles
> squashed dead or still entire, stunned
> like beetles: scattered wingcases and
> legs, heads, appear when the dust settles.
> ('Landscape with Figures').

This is obviously by someone who had read 'The Show' (and another poem, 'Enfidaville', recycles Owen's image of battered religious statues). Douglas had taken over many of Owen's attitudes along with his half-rhymes. Like Rosenberg, he is cool; he expresses little anger or pity, but he takes it for granted that the enemy is a man like himself. In 'Vergissmeinnicht' (forget-me-not; it is significant that he felt free to write in German) he shows that the "killer" had a private life and normal human feelings, and is frank about the ugliness of war. 'How to Kill' is also a frightening poem:

> Now in my dial of glass appears
> the soldier who is going to die.
> He smiles, and moves about in ways
> his mother knows, habits of his.
> The wires touch his face: I cry
> NOW.

As in 'Dulce et Decorum Est', we see the man who is not yet dead, but is about to die. There is nothing any of us can do for him. Moreover

> Being damned, I am amused
> to see the centre of love diffused
> and the waves of love travel into vacancy.

Douglas is not outraged; he seems to be admiring his own skill, but like Owen, who felt that hell was the proper place for soldiers, he calls himself "damned". Men who are to be killed, no doubt for a good reason, still have fiancées and mothers. The poet is prepared to accept his role as killer (there is no passive suffering in these poems) but not to romanticise it.

Some of the young World War II poets simply imitated their predecessors. John Jarmain (killed 1944) wrote in 'Embarkation, 1942':

> In undetected trains we left our land
> At evening secretly, from wayside stations.
> None knew our place of parting; no pale hand
> Waved as we went, not one friend said farewell.
> But grouped on weed-grown platforms
> Only a few officials holding watches
> Noted the stealthy hour of our departing.

This is too obviously inspired by 'The Send-Off' to be good in its own right. But Owen did have one real successor who wrote an impressive poem, 'Cain in the Jungle', first published in 1946:

> I have killed my brother in the jungle;
> Under the green liana's clammy tangle
> I hid, and pressed my trigger, and he died.
>
> Smooth as the spotted panther crept my brother,
> Never a creak of his equipment's leather,
> Never a leaf dislodged nor bird offended.
>
> With his palaeozoic prototype
> My mother shared her own ungainly shape
> In caverns on some slow Silurian stream;
>
> And with the cublings played my father's sons,
> Shoulder to shoulder chipped their flints and bones
> Or scraped a greasy ichthyosaurus hide.
>
> And, when the floods of purple slime receded
> My brother's hutments by the apes were raided,
> I lay beneath my brother's legs and cried.
>
> Yet I have fought my brother for the planets;
> I have never stopped to hear the linnets,
> Or watch the cocos grow against the moon.
>
> I have only slain him in the shadows,
> I have made his slant-eyed women widows
> And inherited his empty meadows.

Little is known about the author, Denys L. Jones, except his date of birth, 1917, but it is clear that he had not only read Owen but learned from him, learned, that is, to use his method in another context. There is the same biblical imagery, the same emphatic half-rhymes, the same deeply compassionate protest (Rosenberg and Douglas are detached by comparison). Even the panther in the second verse may be a descendant of the tigress in 'Strange Meeting'. But in reworking Owen's myth, he has produced something almost as powerful. The speaker has killed a man of another race, probably Japanese, yet they are brothers because they share a common pre-human ancestor. It causes as much grief as if he had killed his real brother (if he does not feel the grief, others will), and recalls the first killing, of Abel by his brother Cain. Time has evolved in a way unknown to Genesis yet the bloodshed continues. Unlike the two men in 'Strange Meeting' there can be no reconciliation, except in fantasy ("I lay beneath my brother's legs and cried"), because this killer is a survivor. He has "only" inherited his brother's "empty meadows", and now sees that the victory was not worth having. It is suggested that the brother, though perhaps also plotting to kill him, lived in harmony with nature, not offending the birds or leaves, while the man who has won does so by ignoring nature to make himself a more efficient killing machine. Like Owen, the poet creates a feeling of over-whelming grief, which leads to protest. If he has "never stopped to hear the linnets", he should have stopped. If the European and the man from the jungle are brothers, then war is a crime against the human family.

There is one other possible instance of Owen's ghost visiting a poet during the Second World War. S.B. Das argues, in *Wilfred Owen's Influence on Three Generations of Poets* (1982), that Eliot might unconsciously have put some of 'Strange Meeting' into his own major work. Certainly Eliot thought Owen a remarkable poet and wrote shortly before his death that 'Strange Meeting' "is of per-manent value and, I think, will never be forgotten, and ... is not only one of the most moving pieces of verse inspired by the war of 1914-18, but also a technical achievement of great originality" (Walsh). Das suggests that the "dead master", or "familiar com-pound ghost" in 'Little Gidding', with whom Eliot has a "strange" encounter, is none other than Owen:

> Between two worlds become much like each other,
> So I find words I never thought to speak
> In streets I never thought I should revisit
> When I left my body on a distant shore.
> Since our concern was speech, and speech impelled us
> To purify the dialect of the tribe
> And urge the mind to aftersight and foresight.

There is no proving it. Eliot had never met Owen in the flesh, and indeed seems to have been thinking of several people, perhaps his "dead master" T.E. Hulme, also killed in the war. But there are correspondences. Both poets had derived the idea of meetings with the dead from Dante. Owen had left his body on a distant shore, poetically speaking, and he too had been concerned with language and wished to purify the 'speech' inherited from the last century:

> For last year's words belong to last year's language
> And next year's words await another voice.

The "two worlds become much like each other" are not only life and death (this is set during the London blitz) but also the century's two great wars. In 'Strange Meeting', Owen had had the "foresight" to guess that this would happen.

But after the Cold War years, war changed. In the Third World, it may still be a matter of whole populations of young men trying to exterminate each other (Iran/Iraq), but in the West the time has long gone when a ruling class will send its sons to fight *en masse*. The American army in Vietnam had disproportionately high numbers of the black, the poor, and those without connections; those who could get out, did. So far from a rush to volunteer, there was a smell of fear all over the campuses (conveyed brilliantly in Cynthia Voigt's 1986 novel *The Runner*) as young people realised they were about to be sacrificed for a doubtful cause. Those who did go produced a remarkable body of poetry, the best of which is collected by W.D. Ehrhart in *Carrying the Darkness* ((1985):

> we have all killed something recently
> we know who owns the night
> and carry darkness with us

in the words of Horace Coleman. They are nearly all survivors (plus the odd woman or draft-dodger), at any rate, there are no dead poets in this collection. But the dead are part of their minds, ringing up, writing on street lamps (scribbling on walls?), tormenting them with memories of lost friends and napalmed children. One of the best poets, John Balaban, writes:

> Our Asian war is over; others have begun.
> Our elders, who tried to mortgage lies,

166

are disgraced, or dead....

In delta swamp in a united Vietnam,
a Marine with a bullfrog for a face,
rots in equatorial heat. An eel
slides through the cage of his bared ribs.
At night, on the old battlefields, ghosts,
like patches of fog, lurk into villages
to maunder on doorsills of cratered homes,
while all across the U.S.A.
the wounded walk about and wonder where to go.
                    ('In Celebration of Spring').

This poetry has many of the same themes as the literature of 1914-18, fear, guilt and homesickness, the impossibility of talking to parents, a feeling of 'what are we doing here?', hostility to civilians:

And what would you do, ma,
if eight of your sons step
out of the TV and begin
killing chickens and burning
hooches in the living room,
stepping on booby traps
and dying in the kitchen?
                    (Steve Hassett, 'Patriot's Day')

Most of it is written in blank, bald, brutal verse, very different from Owen's chiselled metres, and deals in facts — four-letter words, brothels, venereal disease — which he certainly knew about, but seldom mentioned. If he killed anyone, it was in combat, but the Vietnam poets know that they or their friends have murdered prisoners and horribly burned children. Guilt pervades their memories of

that green land
I blackened with my shadow
and the shadow of my flag.
                    (W.D. Ehrhart, 'Letter').

The greenness is constantly remarked on, with lyrical descriptions of rice fields, water buffalo and elephant grass. But it has been desecrated by the military. Ehrhart speaks of when "the last whale is emptied from the sea/ and the last leopard emptied from its skin/ and the last drop of blood refined by Exxon". Writers in the Great War had also talked about what was being done to nature — "the little yellow coltsfoot he had liked so much were all dead with phosgene" (*Death of a Hero*, 3,8). And then there was the problem of reabsorbing the dead in the earth:

> The land cannot hold you all,
> it is filling with debris.
> We will have to ship some home
> for recycling ....
> Rotting into the earth in dusted rows,
> seeping into the earth in chemicals,
> your moisture already lifting into the air
> to rub the dark fire in night mists,
> to cover us with your breath
> while we lay drunken in our camps.
>   (Basil T. Paquet, 'Graves Registration').

Owen, too, had been interested in the earth since boyhood, and having seen what happened to dead bodies at the front he puts this meditation into the mouth of a dying officer in 'A Terre'. The man dreams that spring air might cure him, but knows it is too late:

> Dead men may envy living mites in cheese,
> Or good germs even. Microbes have their joys,
> And subdivide, and never come to death.
> Certainly flowers have the easiest time on earth.
> 'I shall be one with nature, herb and stone',
> Shelley would tell me. Shelley would be stunned:
> The dullest Tommy hugs that fancy now.
> 'Pushing up daisies' is their creed, you know.
>
> To grain, then, go my fat, to buds my sap,
> For all the usefulness there is in soap....
>   Friend, be very sure
> I shall be better off with plants that share
> More peaceably the meadow and the shower.
> Soft rains will touch me, — as they could touch once,

And nothing but the sun shall make me ware.

Owen's vision is the more traditional and less frightening. It has always been a comforting idea that the dead will be reabsorbed by nature (as Shelley said of Keats in *Adonais*), and the soldier expresses this in the pleasant phrase "pushing up daisies". But it is of no comfort to the man in 'A Terre', who passionately wants to live. Once he is dead, he says, he will be lower than specks of dust in the sun, or mites in cheese. He refers to the horror story that the Germans, unwilling to waste anything, boiled dead men to make soap, and concludes that plants know how to live in harmony with nature, while we do not. But according to the American, the land can no longer cope with so many young men being killed at the wrong point in the life cycle, and their corruption will poison the survivors.

The Vietnam experience showed that a war can be stopped if there is a sizeable protest movement and if the army is demoralised. That army certainly was; there were tales of them getting high on drugs, fragging (blowing up) officers and openly saying on film that they were not trying very hard to kill the enemy. These things tend to happen when a war is being lost, and when an army contains a high proportion of conscripts. There were mutinies in all the armies (even the British after the Armistice) in the closing stages of the First World War.

For this reason the 'little' wars of the 1980s and '90s have been fought to a different plan. This is to use high technology against a third world country (so it will be over quickly and at a low cost), and to use only professional soldiers who are unlikely to rebel. (It is also important, as was said above, to soften up public opinion at home). This makes it all the more surprising that one young man in the Falklands task force was outraged by what he was doing; David Tinker (1957-82) was a naval lieutenant who enjoyed his job but did not believe that wars should be fought for reasons of national pride. This probably sprang from a childhood interest in the Great War and its poets

> Rupert Brooke first, then Siegfried Sassoon, then, for a time, Isaac Rosenberg. But always he returned to Wilfred Owen. He applauded Owen's rejection of all the *bullshit* aspects of

war. He cherished Owen's longing for peace instead of war. And in his own writing — whether or not he consciously took Owen as his model — he adopted the same bleak, spare, stripped-down mode of expression. (David Tinker, *A Message from the Falklands* [1982], 20)

In a series of letters home, he described the war as "totally mad.... I cannot think of a single war in Britain's history which has been so pointless.... Not only has Mrs Thatcher survived a political fiasco.... she has become a complete dictator, ordering war without consulting Parliament, and she is dragging the masses, shouting and cheering, behind her. The newspapers just see it as a real-life 'War Mag', and even have drawings of battles, and made-up descriptions, entirely from their own imagination! If some of the horrible ways that people have died occurred in *their* offices maybe they would change their tone" (198). It could have been Owen speaking.

Writing to a school friend, he quoted 'The Next War' from memory:

> Do you remember when we were studying Wilfred Owen at Mill Hill? In his poem where he says, 'Oh death was never enemy of ours.... We whistled while he shaved us with his scythe', he ends up (I'm probably misquoting), 'There'll come a day when men make war on death for lives — not men for flags'. This is what it is, a war for a flag (180).

Owen was still haunting him when he wrote another letter, which eventually made his family decide to commemorate him through a book:

> I sometimes wonder if I am totally odd in that I utterly oppose all this killing that is going on over a flag. Wilfred Owen wrote that 'There'll come a day when men make war on death for lives, not men for flags', but it has been the reverse here — 'nations trek from progress' still (186).

David Tinker was killed on 12 June 1982 — like Wilfred, almost at the end of a war. The poems he had apparently been writing in the South Atlantic were destroyed in the attack on his ship, H.M.S. Glamorgan. He is remembered not for literary reasons but because (as his father wrote afterwards) he too "spoke with the voice of sanity when almost all the eminent, and those who take it on themselves to pronounce on public matters, seem (temporarily, let us hope) to have lost all sense of reality, all sense of proportion".

The other 'little war' of our times — often called the first TV war — was in the Gulf in 1991. Although some soldiers were against it, and said so, the protests most likely to survive came from photographers and war artists, who were allowed in the battle zone under restrictions, and poets, who had to make do with what they saw on screen. John Keane, creator of the painting 'Ecstasy of Fumbling' (the phrase comes from 'Dulce et Decorum Est'), which is dominated by a sinister figure in a gas mask, has kindly allowed me to quote from his diary of 15 February 1991 which describes its genesis:

> The overriding sensation at the moment is, 'What the hell am I doing here?' This question impressed itself profoundly on me yesterday when I went on a facility with 3 hacks and a minder to visit an army field hospital. Innocuous enough, I thought. It was a long, bumpy desert journey in 2 land-rovers. We eventually found the destination, and Bruce, our minder, got out to announce our arrival at the guard tent. A moment later he came running back crying 'Gas gas gas!' Panic! Could this be for real? As I bundled out of the vehicle and looked around everyone seemed to be taking it completely seriously and busily fumbling for their gas masks and Noddy suits. Heart pounding, I did likewise, straining to remember that brief instruction at RAF Innsworth, and hoping that the bundle I had been issued with and religiously carried everywhere contained everything I needed. All the time praying that someone was going to say this was only an exercise, or it had been a false alert. Nobody did. This was a genuine alert. The fumbling continued and I managed to get everything on in the right order. I piled back into the vehicle as instructed, having left my belongings lying in the sand, and we drove a short distance to a spot where we just sat in the car and waited. Trying to control my breathing and contain my claustrophobia, I remained in the back thinking, 'This can't be real', while our driver and Kate Adie sat in front. We stayed like that while Kate

said ominous things like, 'So this is war', and seemed desperate to get out and do some filming. After some minutes I relaxed a little and reached for my video camera to capture some of the worst moments of my life on tape.

The picture was created with the help of video stills. John Keane writes, "It was important for me to attempt to describe this event somehow in paint on canvas, not just because it was disturbing for myself, but also because the lingering threat of possible gas attack was ever-present in the minds of those involved throughout the Gulf War. I have been familiar with the poetry of Wilfred Owen since I was introduced to it at school, and the phrase 'ecstasy of fumbling' presented itself as an obvious title, not only because of the aptness of description, but also because it conjures the ghastly anachronism of the notion of chemical warfare — something I had previously thought had long since been declared unacceptable, something associated only with the distant horrors of the First World War".

It will be seen that John Keane had an experience very like Owen's and so was able to send "dispatches from the front". But poets are unlikely to be found in modern armies, and therefore have to use their imagination and such visual aids as they can find. "High Tech wars drain all poetry from the world", writes the poet Peter Porter; "they become video games leaving only charred bodies behind. Even Shakespeare could do nothing with Baghdad and smart bombs" (*Times Literary Supplement*, 15 March 1992). Tony Harrison's 'A Cold Coming' is an attempt to grapple with this problem. It is based on Kenneth Jarecke's photograph of a dreadfully burned Iraqi, which he links with the rumour that three American soldiers had frozen their sperm so that if necessary they could have children after death. That seems grotesquely inappropriate, until you realise that the technology which enabled them to bank sperm also made it possible to crush a third world country with the minimum loss of life on 'our' side. The 'enemy' dead, who numbered at least a hundred thousand, were practically erased from public consciousness because, as Owen said, "they were not ours". The only way a western poet can cross that gulf ('gulf' seems an appropriate word) is to make the dead speak:

I saw the charred Iraqi lean
towards me from bomb-blasted screen....

as though he'd stopped to ask the way
and this is what I heard him say:

'Don't be afraid I've picked on you
for this exclusive interview.

Isn't it your sort of poet's task
to find words for this frightening mask?...

'So press RECORD! I want to reach
the warring nations with my speech'.

As one critic pointed out, there is a long tradition in Western poetry (Virgil, Dante, Eliot, Owen) of encounters between dead and living, in which the dead pass on their new-found wisdom. Tony Harrison has obviously been influenced by 'Strange Meeting' but, it seems, does not totally endorse it. The corpse says:

'Lie that you saw me and I smiled
to see the soldier hug his child.

Lie and pretend that I excuse
my bombing by B52s,

pretend I pardon and forgive
that they still do and I don't live....

Pretend I've got the imagination
to see the world beyond one nation.

That's your job, poet, to pretend
I want my foe to be my friend'.

What I think Harrison is saying is that the world has changed since Owen's war, when two vast armies fought each other to a standstill and both sides clearly had a common interest in stopping it. Then it was possible to imagine two men from warring nations being reconciled after death. The situation is different when one side eliminates the other in a 'turkey shoot' and then goes home to wave

173

flags:

> Stars and Stripes in sticky paws
> may sow the seeds for future wars.

Photographs of the returning soldier hugging his child, such as we always see after victories, encourage us to forget what he has been doing away from the camera. It is still the poet's job to be truthful, but he is not now a soldier seeking reconciliation but a non-combatant seeking to draw attention to the victims. Tony Harrison — who, of course, had not 'been there' — has been accused of trivialising the dead man by putting his own words in his mouth. Obviously the poem could not exist without the photograph, and I do not say that it is as good as 'Strange Meeting'. But photographic images are now part of our consciousness, and can spark off poems which have value. They are anyway the only kind of war poems likely to be written in English now; if another Owen appeared, it would have to be in another part of the world. Like the film *The Killing Fields*, which is about two friends, an American and a Cambodian, they do at least show the enormous gap between the third world and ourselves.

Do such poems have an effect? Owen feared they did not. So did the American Hayden Carruth, who pointed out that he had spent thirty years writing them:

> and not one
> breath was restored
> to one
> shattered throat
> mans womans or childs
> not one not
> one
> but death went on and on
> ('On Being Asked to Write a Poem Against the War in
> Vietnam').

On the other hand, changing even one mind is a trek towards progress, of a sort.

Building bridges, breaking ranks

Around the end of 1917, Owen had written a poem apparently addressed to Sassoon and urging him not to go back to the war. Its resemblance to 'Strange Meeting' is obvious:

> Earth's wheels run oiled with blood. Forget we that.
> Let us lie down and dig ourselves in thought....
>
> Let us forgo men's minds that are brutes' natures.
> Let us not sup the blood which some say nurtures.
>
> Be we not swift with swiftness of the tigress;
> Let us break ranks and we will trek from progress.
>
> Miss we the march of this retreating world
> Into old citadels that are not walled.
>
> Then when their blood hath clogged their chariot wheels
> We will go up and wash them from deep wells
>
> What though we sink from men as pitchers falling
> Many shall raise us up to be their filling
>
> Even from wells we sunk too deep for war ....

The poem belongs to a time when, as one observer said, there had been a "deliberate poisoning of the wells of human feeling" (Douglas Goldring, *Reputations* [1920], 82) and there was a general belief that "blood nurtures", as I argued in the section on Yeats. Owen does not hope to be able to change this immediately but he urges those who think like him, especially poets, to "break ranks", drop out of society and return only when it is ready to listen. They will sink out of sight for a while, but many will turn to their message ("raise us up to be their filling") in years to come. In a sense, this has happened, but in 1918 it was very difficult for a young man to drop out. The military machine had first claim on him. So, a few months later, when Owen incorporated this poem into 'Strange Meeting', the positives had become negatives; instead of "let us break ranks" we find "none will break ranks", which sounds very like despair. Sassoon had gone back and he was about to do so. Ever since, people have asked why.

He told his mother that it was for the sake of "his boys" (this was not a personal bond, as he did not know the men he was going back to be with). To Sassoon, he said it might be good for his poetry. In modern times, now that the 'cowardice' story has surfaced, we may think he went back to "get some reputation of gallantry". Probably it was a mixture of all these motives, a feeling that he could not stand aside from the enormous tragedy of his time. Then, it seemed a responsible and selfless act; today, it may seem a cop-out. A contemporary poet, Judith Kazantzis, accuses him and Sassoon of staying "submissive to the high-minded macho ethic of the English officer" (*Scars Upon My Heart* [ed. Catherine Reilly, 1981], xviii). She continues this argument in a poem dedicated to Wilfred Owen and David Tinker:

> 'All a poet can do today is warn'.
> With what caught pride does the young
> officer draw up to his peaked cap.
> In the photograph
> Owen smiles with his expressive
> eyes and his plump cheeks. In the next,
> a glad, rangy face, fair hair,
> David Tinker, Lieut. RN, on board, ploughing
> the South Atlantic, at first ardent,
> then writing home, 'the professional forces
> of both sides' — he was one —
> 'do what they are told. If two
> megalomaniac idiots tell them
> to beat each other's brains out they do'.

Her poem — which is of its time, the 1980s and the Greenham peace camp, as clearly as Sassoon's 'Death's Brotherhood' is of his — urges the young men to turn against the "megalomaniac idiots" in power:

> But you say: Orders are orders.
> But you say: I cannot leave my men, my brothers.
> But you say: Now this is my only life
> so has to be my death.
> No one at home can know our deep bonds.
> I shout back through the dumb wood

across the bloody channels:
Whip vines or gossamer, what garland ties
you to your killing post?
                    ('For example Owen').

One man did "break ranks" in the last year of the war. Max
Plowman, a future secretary of the Peace Pledge Union and friend
of Orwell, attempted to resign his commission and was court-martialled at just about the time Wilfred was telling his brother that
he intended to go back and be killed. In his statement Plowman
said that he was no longer prepared to kill men he knew nothing
about, and "if it is said that the middle of the war is no fit time to
come to such a conclusion, I reply that every moment is opportune
in which to cease to do evil and learn to do well". To my knowledge
he was the only British serviceman of 1914-18 who refused to go
on fighting and did not change his mind. He was found guilty but
discharged, which suggests that the 'impossible' can sometimes
be achieved.

Wilfred probably never heard of this protest and, for reasons
gone into earlier, I believe it would not have changed his decision.
He might have broken ranks, perhaps, if hundreds or thousands
of other men had been doing so; as things were, he was dragged
back, like Sassoon, Mackintosh, and the rest, by psychological
bonds. "The 1914-18 war was too much for Wilfred Owen", wrote
Alun Lewis, before dying in a later war; "there was too much
against him, and he was too much alone with his love of humanity
and his hatred of the authorities who legalised the crucifixion. But
slowly, this is my fantasy, we are achieving wisdom" ('Last Pages
of a Long Journal').

Is it a fantasy? Certainly Owen and others helped to make things
easier for those who came after them. Many conscientious objectors
died as a result of their treatment in the First World War; in the
Second, they were treated much better. During the Vietnam war
thousands of Americans broke ranks and refused to fight. In Serbia,
in the early 1990s, great numbers of young men are still doing so.

There is a better ideal than the blood-brotherhood between
fighting men, and that is the 'international idea' in which people
of different nations and cultures seek to find common ground.
Owen's weaker poems, 'Apologia' and 'Greater Love', have al-

ways been popular with those who have been through the ranks, but it is 'Strange Meeting' which has universal appeal. Today, everyone agrees in theory that we are one world and must solve our problems together. But even in the heart of Europe, the demons of nationalism fight on.

I come back to where the First World War started, in Bosnia. Here the Yugoslav Ivo Andric, born a few months before Wilfred, was inspired to write one of the great novels of the twentieth century, *Na Drini cuprija* (1945), *The Bridge on the Drina*. It tells the story not of a man but of a bridge, built in the middle ages to link east and west. For hundreds of years people of different races and traditions come together on this bridge, but in August 1914 it is blown up and human bonds are destroyed with it:

> That wild beast, which lives in man and does not dare to show itself until the barriers of law and custom have been removed, was now set free. The signal was given, the barriers were down. As has so often happened in the history of man, permission was tacitly granted for acts of violence and plunder, even for murder, if they were carried out in the name of higher interests, according to established rules, and against a limited number of men of a particular type and belief. A man who saw clearly and with open eyes and was then living could see how this miracle took place and how the whole of a society could, in a single day, be transformed. (Chapter 22).

Wilfred, who was living then and saw clearly what was happening, would have understood the symbolism of the bridge. Ivo Andric's message also makes sense to those who have seen the present-day tragedy of Yugoslavia — "our destiny on this earth lies in the struggle against decay, death and dissolution ... men must persevere in this struggle, even if it were completely in vain" (Chapter 5). Progress is not a straight line; we trek from it, or towards it, in each generation.

Wilfred Owen is commemorated, not by the traditional statue, but by a modern sculpture which shows a pattern of trenches and bridges, joined. It is a good symbol of what his poetry has come to mean for us. His chance to build bridges of another kind was lost on the Sambre canal in the dying days of the 1914-18 war.

Bibliography

Abbreviations

Blunden: *The Poems of Wilfred Owen*, edited with a Memoir and Notes by Edmund Blunden (Chatto & Windus, London, 1931)

Casebook: Dominic Hibberd (ed.), *Poetry of the First World War: A Casebook* (Macmillan, London, 1981)

C.L.: Wilfred Owen, *Collected Letters*, ed. Harold Owen and John Bell (Oxford University Press, 1967)

D.H.: Dominic Hibberd, *Owen the Poet* (Macmillan, London, 1986)

J.F.O.: Harold Owen, *Journey from Obscurity: Wilfred Owen 1893-1918*, three volumes, (Oxford University Press, 1963-5)

S.J.: *Siegfried's Journey 1916-20* (Faber & Faber, London, 1945)

Stallworthy: Jon Stallworthy, *Wilfred Owen* (Oxford University Press, 1974)

Welland: D.S.R. Welland, *Wilfred Owen: A Critical Study(Chatto & Windus, London, 1960)*

Further Reading

Sven Backman, *Tradition Transformed: Studies in the Poetry of Wilfred Owen* (Liber Läromedal, Gleerup, Lund, 1979)

S.B. Das, *Wilfred Owen's Influence on Three Generations of Poets* (Roy & Roy, India, 1982)

W.D. Ehrhart (ed.), *Carrying the Darkness, American Indochina: The Poetry of the Vietnam War* (Avon, New York, 1985)

Paul Fussell, *The Great War and Modern Memory* (Oxford University Press, 1975)

Brian Gardner (ed.), *Up the Line to Death: The War Poets 1914-18, An Anthology* (Methuen, London, 1964)

Brian Gardner (ed.), *The Terrible Rain: The War Poets 1939-1945* (Methuen, London, 1966)

Desmond Graham, *The Truth of War: Owen, Blunden, Rosenberg* (Carcanet, Manchester, 1984)

Robert Graves, *Goodbye to All That* (Cape, London, 1929)

Dominic Hibberd, *Wilfred Owen: The Last Year* (Constable, London,

1992)

Catherine Reilly (ed.), *Scars upon my Heart: Women's Poetry and Verse of the First World War* (Virago, London, 1981)

Jon Silkin, *Out of Battle: The Poetry of the Great War* (Oxford University Press, 1972)

Kenneth Simcox, *Wilfred Owen: Anthem for a Doomed Youth* (Woburn Press, London, 1987)

T.J. Walsh, *A Tribute to Wilfred Owen* (Birkenhead Institute [private printing], 1964)

Robert Wohl, *The Generation of 1914* (Wiednfeld & Nicholson, London, 1979)

Series Afterword

The Border country is that region between England and Wales which is upland and lowland, both and neither. Centuries ago kings and barons fought over these Marches without their national allegiance ever being settled. In our own time, referring to his own childhood, that eminent borderman Raymond Williams once said: "We talked of 'The English' who were not us, and 'The Welsh' who were not us". It is beautiful, gentle, intriguing, and often surprising. It displays majestic landscapes, which show a lot, and hide some more. People now walk it, poke into its cathedrals and bookshops, and fly over or hang-glide from its mountains, yet its mystery remains.

In cultural terms the region is as fertile as (in parts) its agriculture and soil. The continued success of the Three Choirs Festival and the growth of the border town of Hay as a centre for the second-hand book trade have both attracted international recognition. The present series of introductory books is offered in the light of such events. Writers as diverse as Mary Webb, Raymond Williams and Wilfred Owen are seen in the special light — perhaps that cloudy, golden twilight so characteristic of the region — of their origin in this area or association with it. There are titles too, though fewer, on musicians and painters. The Gloucestershire composers such as Samuel Sebastian Wesley, and painters like David Jones, bear an imprint of border woods, rivers, villages and hills.

How wide is the border? Two, five or fifteen miles each side of the boundary; it depends on your perspective, on the placing of the nearest towns, on the terrain itself, and on history. In the time of Offa and after, Hereford itself was a frontier town, and Welsh was spoken there even in the nineteenth century. True border folk traditionally did not recognise those from even a few miles away. Today, with greater mobility, the crossing of boundaries is easier, whether for education, marriage, art or leisure. For myself, who spent some childhood years in Herefordshire and a decade of middle-age crossing between England and Wales once a week, I can only say that as you approach the border you feel it. Suddenly you are in that finally elusive terrain, looking from a bare height down onto a plain, or from the lower land up to a gap in the hills, and you want to explore it, maybe not to return.

This elusiveness pertains to the writers and artists too. It is often difficult to decide who is border, to what extent and with what impact on their work. The urbane Elizabeth Barrett Browning, prominent figure in the salons of London and Italy in her time, spent virtually all her life until her late twenties just outside Ledbury in Herefordshire, and this fact is being seen by current critics and scholars as of more and more significance. The twentieth century 'English pastoral' composers — with names like Parry, Howells and Vaughan-Williams — were nearly all border people. One wonders whether border country is now suddenly found on the English side of the Severn Bridge, and how far even John Milton's *Comus*, famous for its first production at Ludlow Castle, is in any sense such a work. Then there is the fascinating Uxbridge-born Peggy Whistler, transposed in the 1930s into Margiad Evans to write her (epilepsis-based) visionary novels set near her adored Ross-on-Wye and which today still retain a magical charm. Further north: could Barbara Pym, born and raised in Oswestry, even remotely be called a border writer? Most people would say that the poet A.E. Housman was far more so, yet he hardly ever visited the county after which his chief book of poems, *A Shropshire Lad*, is named. Further north still: there is the village of Chirk on the boundary itself, where R.S. Thomas held his first curacy; there is Gladstone's Hawarden library, just outside Chester and actually into Clwyd in Wales itself; there is intriguingly the Wirral town of Birkenhead, where Wilfred Owen spent his adolescence and where his fellow war poet the Welsh Eisteddfod winner Hedd Wyn was awarded his chair — posthumously.

On the Welsh side the names are different. The mystic Ann Griffiths; the metaphysical poet Henry Vaughan; the astonishing nineteenth century symbolist Arthur Machen (in Linda Dowling's phrase, "Pater's prose as registered by Wilde"); and the remarkable Thomas Olivers of Gregynog, associated with the writing of the well-known hymn 'Lo He comes with clouds descending'.

Those descending clouds...; in border country the scene hangs overhead, and it is easy to indulge in unwarranted speculation. Most significant perhaps is the difference to the two peoples on either side. From England, the border meant the enticement of emptiness, a strange unpopulated land, going up and up into the hills. From Wales, the border meant the road to London, to the university, or to employment, whether by droving sheep, or later to the industries of Birmingham and Liverpool. It also meant the enemy, since borders and boundaries are necessarily political. Much is shared, yet different languages are spoken, in more than one sense.

With certain notable exceptions, the books in this series are short introductory studies of one person's work or some aspect of it. There are no footnotes or indexes. The bibliography lists main sources referred to into the text, and sometimes others, for anyone who would like to pursue the topic further. The authors reflect the diversity of their subjects. They are specialists or academics; critics or biographers; poets or musicians themselves; or ordinary people with however an established reputation of writing imaginatively and directly about what moves them. They are of various ages, both sexes, Welsh and English, border people themselves or from further afield.

To those who explore the matter, the subjects — the writers, painters and composers written about — seem increasingly to be united by a particular kind of vision. This holds good however diverse they are in other, main ways; and of course they are diverse indeed. One might scarcely associate, it would seem, Raymond Williams with Samuel Sebastian Wesley, or Dennis Potter with Thomas Traherne. But one has to be careful in such assumptions. The epigraph to Bruce Chatwin's twentieth century novel *On the Black Hill* is a passage from the seventeenth century mystic writer Jeremy Taylor. Thomas Traherne himself is subject of a recent American study which puts Traherne's writings into dialogue with the European philosopher-critics Martin Heidegger, Jaques Derrida and Jaques Lacan. And the current bestselling writer of thrillers, Ellis Peters, sets her stories in a Shrewsbury of the late medieval Church with a cunning quiet monk as her ever-engaging sleuth.

The vision (name incidentally of the farmhouse in Chatwin's

novel) is something to do with the curious border light already mentioned. To avoid getting sentimental and mystic here — though border writers have at times been both — one might suggest literally that this effect is meteorological. Maybe the sun's rays are refracted through skeins of dew or mist that hit the stark mountains and low hills at curious ascertainable angles, with prismatic results. Not that rainbows are the point in our area: it is more the contrasts of gold, green and grey. Some writers never mention it. They don't have to. But all the artists of the region see it, are affected by it, and transpose their highly different emana- tions of reality through its transparencies. Meanwhile, on the ground, the tourist attractions draw squads from diverse cultural and ethnic origins; agriculture enters the genetic-engineering age; New Age travellers are welcome and unwelcome; and the motor- way runs parallel past all —"Lord of the M5", as the poet Geoffrey Hill has dubbed the Saxon king Offa, he of the dyke that bisects the region where it can still be identified. The region has its uniqueness, then, and a statistically above-average number of writers and artists (we have identified over fifty clear candidates so far) have drawn something from it, which it is the business of the present series to elucidate.

Wilfred Owen was killed at the age of twenty-five, so that — as it happens — most of his life was spent in the border region. Perhaps that is partly why his poems and letters savour the different borderness of the No-Man's-Land of wartime's front- line, not that the analogy can be pursued too far. The name of Wilfred Owen would probably be most British people's first choice if asked to exemplify the term 'war poet'. He was born in 1893, so that this study by Merryn Williams marks his first centenary, an event celebrated this year all over the country in many ways and locations. The recently founded Wilfred Owen Association, based in Shrewsbury, is to the forefront of these events. A feature of Merryn Williams's book is its emphasis on a sad irony, namely, that Owen has had all too numerous successors in the twentieth century, and all too many occasions for his subject to receive further treatment. The pity of war goes on, not least in Sarajevo, where Owen's war started.

John Powell Ward

Acknowledgements

The publisher gratefully acknowledges the following:

Bloodaxe Books for permission to reprint extracts from The Gaze of Gorgon by Tony Harrison (Bloodaxe Books, 1992)

George Simon for permission to quote from 'They', 'Sick Leave' and 'The Stint' by Siegfried Sassoon

The English Faculty Library, Oxford for photographs 1, 2, 3, 4, 7, 8

The Fitzwilliam Museum, Cambridge for photograph 6

The Cartoon Study Centre, University of Kent, Canterbury for photograph 11

John Keane for photograph 12